Mastering Google Appsheet

:

FROM BEGINNER TO PRO

By Daniel Melehi

Revised April 2025 Edition

©2025

Contents

Introduction

Hi, I'm Daniel, and I remember when I first started using Google AppSheet. I was both excited and overwhelmed by all the possibilities it offered. The idea of creating custom apps without writing a single line of code felt almost magical. Yet, like many others, I wondered where to begin. That sense of curiosity and uncertainty became the foundation of my journey into app creation, data management, and automation—a journey that inspired me to write this book.

Welcome to *Mastering Google AppSheet: from Beginner to Pro*. In this book, we'll explore how to transform your ideas into a functional application step by step. Whether you're completely new to AppSheet or have some experience with spreadsheets and data organization, I hope to guide you in transforming raw concepts into powerful apps.

I can recall spending hours trying to understand how to refine my data sources, set up basic tables, and configure user interfaces. Over time, I discovered shortcuts, best practices, and essential tips that I'm eager to share with you. Together, we'll dive into each aspect of AppSheet, from structuring your data and designing elegant forms to incorporating smart formulas and ensuring top-notch security.

In writing this book, I kept in mind the moments when I stumbled as a beginner, as well as the times I celebrated breakthrough solutions. My goal is for you to walk away feeling comfortable with Google AppSheet's features and inspired to unleash your creativity through custom apps. By combining accessible steps with practical examples, I believe this journey will be both informative and fun. If you're ready to turn your ideas into mobile or web applications, let's get started on this adventure together!

Chapter 1: Understanding Google AppSheet Basics

GETTING ACQUAINTED WITH APPSHEET

Welcome to this chapter, in this chapter, I'd like to introduce you to the core concepts that make **Google AppSheet** such an exciting tool. When I first discovered AppSheet, I was struck by the idea of creating complete applications straight from my data without delving into complex coding. I quickly realized how it could radically transform how I managed tasks, collaborated with others, and turned simple spreadsheets into dynamic apps.

At its heart, AppSheet is a platform that allows you to design, build, and deploy business applications in a matter of minutes. Instead of obsessing over programming languages, you focus on your *data* and the *experience* your users will have. This simplicity is what makes AppSheet so approachable to beginners, but don't mistake that for lack of power. With the right structure, you'll find that AppSheet can handle anything from a simple list-tracking tool to sophisticated, multi-layered applications.

WHY A NO-CODE SOLUTION?

You might be wondering, "Why choose a no-code platform over traditional development?" When I first started, I questioned whether no-code approaches could really keep up with ever-shifting requirements. But as I experimented, I learned that **no-code tools** like AppSheet excel at rapid development, iterative testing, and real-time collaboration. These qualities make it a game-changer for teams or individuals looking to streamline processes without waiting for a professional developer to step in.

Key advantages of using AppSheet:

- Fast Prototyping – Build an MVP (Minimum Viable Product) in hours, not weeks.
- User-Focused – Effortlessly tailor the interface to fit your audience's needs.
- Cost-Effective – Lower development and maintenance costs, since you handle it visually instead of hiring large teams.
- Scalable Solutions – Start small and grow as your user base expands.

Of course, if you do require specialized features, AppSheet provides ways to integrate with external services or incorporate custom logic. But for the majority of typical business workflows—like managing inventory, conducting surveys, or tracking project tasks—AppSheet's built-in functionalities will often suffice.

CORE COMPONENTS AT A GLANCE

To fully grasp how AppSheet brings your application ideas to life, let's look at its foundational building blocks. You can think of these components as puzzle pieces that interlock to form your final product.

Component	Role
Data	This is the heart of your app—often in the form of cloud spreadsheets, databases, or files.
UX Layer	Controls how your app looks and feels, including layouts, themes, and navigation.
Logic & Behavior	Defines how your app reacts to user inputs. This includes forms, workflows, and formulas.
Security & Access	Manages who can view, edit, or share data, ensuring only the right people have access.

When I first started working with AppSheet, I often got these components mixed up. With time, I realized that understanding each one and how they interact is the key to building effective applications. A clear mental picture of these core parts will save you a lot of confusion down the line.

HOW EVERYTHING FITS TOGETHER

My first few AppSheet projects were simple: a personal task manager with a table of tasks and some quick visual customization. Even with that barebones approach, I saw how each component worked in harmony. I'd update a row in my spreadsheet, which would then update in real time within the app. Formulas let me automate notifications for due dates, and I could adjust security settings to share the app with my close friends.

If you imagine your application like a carefully crafted system, the data is the information flowing beneath the surface, while the UX layer is the friendly face your audience sees. Logic ties it all together, ensuring every user action leads to the correct outcome. Meanwhile, security measures keep unwanted eyes away. Grasping this synergy is the essence of understanding Google AppSheet basics.

In the chapters that follow, we'll expand on each area, but if you can keep these fundamental ideas in mind—**Data**, **UX Layer**, **Logic**, and **Security**—you'll have a solid base for building powerful, user-friendly applications.

Chapter 2: Setting Up Your AppSheet Account

CREATING YOUR APPSHEET PROFILE

Welcome to this chapter, I remember that moment when I realized how crucial it was to configure my AppSheet account properly. Back then, the excitement of diving into app creation sometimes tempted me to rush this process. But believe me, spending a few extra minutes to set everything up right will save you hours of potential confusion later.

To get started, you'll need a **Google account** (or another supported provider like Microsoft or Dropbox). The registration process is straightforward: simply navigate to the AppSheet website, click the sign-up button, and follow the prompts to grant necessary permissions. I found it liberating to know that once I authorized AppSheet, all my relevant Google Drive or Microsoft OneDrive resources became instantly accessible within the platform.

CONNECTING CLOUD SERVICES

Once you've created your profile, it's time to connect the cloud services that house your *data*. For many of us, that's Google Drive; however, AppSheet also works wonderfully with other storage options, such as Box or Dropbox. When I did this step for the first time, I was amazed at how AppSheet immediately scanned my folders for potential data sources. If you've organized your spreadsheets well, you'll soon see the makings of your next app come to life.

Cloud Service	Key Advantages
Google Drive	Native integration, real-time syncing with Sheets
Microsoft OneDrive	Seamless connection with Excel files
Dropbox	Flexibility to manage files outside of typical suites

Tip: It's wise to keep your spreadsheets in a dedicated folder, so you don't mix work-in-progress data with unrelated files. This organizational habit will help you navigate your file structure more cleanly.

ORGANIZING APPSHEET SETTINGS

After granting permissions and linking your preferred cloud services, you'll likely want to customize how AppSheet handles your data. Early on, I neglected this step and ended up scrambling to manage permissions for different users. From my experience, set up **default sharing** options and **access rules** right at the beginning. You'll find these under your account's Settings or Security sections, where you can:

- Adjust access levels for collaborators—ideal if you're building an app with a team.
- Enable features like **auto-sync**, so your users always see the latest data.
- Explore advanced options, such as **data partitioning** or integrations with enterprise tools, if you anticipate large-scale usage.

When I started, I found that meticulously assigning the right role to each collaborator prevented conflicting edits and ensured everyone had the correct level of access. For instance, you might have some team members who need read-only privileges for data integrity, while others require full administrative capabilities.

EXPLORING PLAN OPTIONS

Before you finalize your account setup, be sure to review AppSheet's **subscription plans**. Although the free plan is more than adequate for simple personal projects, you may want to upgrade if you start collaborating heavily or require premium features like enhanced security or advanced automation. I still recall the aha moment when I realized that investing in a higher-tier plan was well worth it— particularly if you're aiming to build a business-critical application.

My personal rule of thumb: Always try a proof-of-concept on the free plan first. Then, if you see real value in scaling up, that's your cue to move to a paid subscription. This incremental approach ensures you don't pay for features you don't need early on.

WRAPPING UP YOUR ACCOUNT SETUP

By now, you should have a fully functioning AppSheet account with easy access to your favorite cloud services and the right collaborators in place. Take one quick pass through your settings to confirm all is in order—this extra diligence has saved me from headaches more times than I can count. After this, you'll be ready to create your very first app with confidence and clarity.

In the next chapter, we'll explore the AppSheet interface itself, giving you a guided tour of the menus, panels, and features essential for building and managing your apps effectively. You're about to enter the heart of AppSheet, where ideas become realities faster than you can imagine!

Chapter 3: Navigating the AppSheet Interface

OVERVIEW OF THE MAIN EDITOR

Welcome to this chapter, I remember the moment I first opened AppSheet's Editor. It felt like stepping into a workshop filled with all sorts of tools and controls. At first glance, there's a lot to see—panels, tabs, preview screens, and menus—but trust me, once you've learned your way around, this environment becomes your creative playground. In this section, I'll show you how I like to navigate this interface to work quickly and efficiently.

When you open the Editor, you'll typically see a main workspace with panels on either side and a live preview somewhere in the center or to the right. What I find so convenient is that each panel focuses on a specific part of your app—be it data, design, or settings—allowing you to make quick adjustments without losing sight of the bigger picture. It's almost as if you have a team of specialist panels waiting to help shape your app the moment you click on them.

THE LEFT-HAND MENU

If you look to the left side of the Editor, you'll notice a vertical menu that groups different features into sections. This is one of my favorite spots to explore because it acts like a roadmap. Each button here corresponds to a core part of your app: Data, UX, Behaviors, Automation, and so on. I suggest starting with the Data section to confirm your tables are set up correctly before moving on to design and more advanced features.

- **Data:** Manage tables, slices, and columns for your app here.
- **UX:** Customize layouts, themes, and how your data is presented.
- **Behavior:** Configure actions, workflows, and automation triggers.
- **Security:** Set who can access what data, ensuring privacy.

Navigating these sections is straightforward: just click a tab, and the central content area will update to match. Early on, I made a habit of hopping between Data and UX to see how a change in a table or column would reflect instantly in the app's interface. This gave me both reassurance and a real-time testing environment for my ideas.

CENTRAL WORKSPACE AND TABS

My favorite feature: the central workspace is where the majority of your customization magic happens. After selecting a section from the left-hand menu, you'll notice a series of tabs or subheadings across the top of this workspace. For instance, in the UX section, you'll see choices like "Views," "Brand," and "Format Rules." You can think of each tab as a small laboratory dedicated to a particular aspect of your app.

Let's say you're working on "Views." You'll be able to pick from many view types—like decks, tables, calendars, or maps—and define how you want your users to see or interact with data. It's a simple click-based adaptation process: select a view type, assign it to a table, and give it a friendly name. Watching how these changes appear immediately in the sample app on the right side is both thrilling and incredibly helpful in validating design choices.

PREVIEW AND APP EMULATOR

On the right side or at the bottom (depending on your screen size and personal preference) you'll find the Preview or Emulator. In my opinion, this is where the real excitement lies, because this live preview shows you exactly how your app looks and behaves on a mobile device or browser. When I first started, I used to make changes and then constantly switch to my phone to see how it looked. The integrated emulator saves you time by reflecting changes immediately, right there on your screen.

If you click the gear icon within the preview, you can switch between tablet, phone, and desktop views. Testing each mode is invaluable for ensuring your app is engaging and functional across devices—something I overlooked in my early attempts, only to find out that my layout was skewed on phones. Checking all the views right here saves you the hassle of discovering issues later on.

ESSENTIAL ACTION BUTTONS

One small detail that often goes unnoticed is the set of action buttons along the top or bottom of the Editor. These include options to **Save**, **Regenerate**, **Preview**, and sometimes **Manage** your app. Here's what they generally do:

Button	Purpose
Save	Commits your changes to the app so you can test them live.
Regenerate	Updates the column structure if you modify your data's schema.
Preview	Loads an updated view in the emulator, reflecting the latest edits.

Manage	Provides an overview of deployment settings, version control, and performance metrics.

I learned that hitting "Save" before switching sections can prevent unexpected behavior—especially if you're experimenting with multiple features at once. The "Regenerate" button, on the other hand, is a lifesaver when you add or remove columns from your underlying spreadsheet. It ensures AppSheet stays in sync with your evolving data.

STAYING ORGANIZED

In these early stages, it's easy to get carried away clicking multiple UX configurations, toggling behaviors, and adding tables. Take my advice: maintain a logical sequence when you navigate. I usually start by confirming all my tables are correct, then move on to creating views, and finally tackle any automation or custom behaviors. This structured approach keeps the interface tidy and makes it less likely that you'll lose track of your place after exploring multiple layers.

Pro tip: Give your views meaningful names. It might sound trivial, but once you start to accumulate several, looking at a list of "View 1," "View 2," "View 3" can be confusing. Labels like "Project List," "Order Form," or "Client Map" keep everything clear and consistent.

EXPLORING ADDITIONAL PANELS

Besides the core interface sections, you might spot additional panels or popup dialogues for advanced settings. These typically appear when you select specialized options like row-specific format rules or quick-edit fields. Although these supplemental windows can seem intimidating at first, they focus on the details that make your app more polished, so don't be shy about clicking around. Each panel usually comes with embedded hints to guide you through the configuration process.

Overall, navigating the AppSheet interface is a blend of organized exploration and quick experimentation. Once you understand how the panels, tabs, and emulator connect, it's much easier to bring your ideas to life. This environment is designed to give you immediate feedback, so you can refine your app in real time and eventually head into deeper customization without missing a beat.

Take a breath, have fun exploring, and remember that every button, tab, and preview mode exists to help you shape the user experience. With this strong foundation in navigating AppSheet's Editor, you're ready to fine-tune and expand your apps with confidence.

Chapter 4: Creating Your First App

PLANNING YOUR APP CONCEPT

Welcome to this chapter, I remember the thrill I felt the very first time I decided to build an app from scratch using Google AppSheet. My mind buzzed with ideas, but I quickly learned that jumping in without a plan can lead to confusion. Spending a few moments brainstorming your app's purpose, potential users, and required data goes a long way.

Let's say you want to create a simple task manager or a small inventory system. Think about what data you'll need to track and how you envision users interacting with that data. Will the app be for a single person or a larger team? Do you need the ability to add photos, locations, or specific notes? These questions help shape your initial setup and keep you focused on exactly what the app should accomplish.

PREPARING YOUR SPREADSHEET

Because AppSheet thrives on data, a well-organized spreadsheet is usually the best place to start. You can use

Google Sheets, Excel, or another supported format. In my early attempts, I discovered that neat column headers and consistent data types (like dates, text fields, or numeric entries) make AppSheet's intelligent features work more smoothly.

Here's how I typically set up my spreadsheet:

- *Header Row:* Label columns clearly (e.g., "Task Name," "Due Date," "Status") to help AppSheet automatically detect the column purpose.
- *Data Types:* Keep text-only cells separate from numeric or date fields so it's easier to create forms later.
- *Sample Rows:* Add a few example entries to see how your app interprets the data right away.

Once you have your spreadsheet organized, you're poised to bring it to life in the AppSheet environment.

CREATING A NEW APP IN APPSHEET

With your data ready, it's time for the exciting moment—creating your first app! Head to the AppSheet homepage and you'll find an option to "Start with your own data." Click that, select your spreadsheet, and watch as AppSheet automatically scans your data to build a basic version of your app.

When I first saw my sample data transformed into a real, clickable interface, it felt almost magical. One of my favorite aspects of AppSheet is how quickly a simple list of rows and columns can turn into a functional application. Even if everything isn't polished yet, this auto-generated structure sets a strong foundation to build upon.

ADJUSTING THE AUTO-GENERATED VIEWS

A personal tip: Don't be surprised if the initial layout isn't exactly what you had in mind. AppSheet makes an educated guess about the best way to display your data—often a table view or a card-like interface. This is your chance to step into the Editor and refine.

In the Editor, navigate to the "UX" section and you'll see various default views. For example, if you're creating a task-tracking app, you may see a "Tasks" view that shows a table of everything, possibly a "Detail" view for each individual entry, and a "Form" view for adding or editing tasks. Feel free to experiment here—rename the views, pick different view types, and reorder them so the most important screen appears first.

CONFIGURING BASIC APP BEHAVIOR

Next, head over to "Behavior" or "Automation" sections to adjust how your new app behaves. Maybe you want your app to automatically send a reminder email when a due date is close, or to confirm user input with a quick message. Even if you don't add automation right away, exploring these settings will open your eyes to the possibilities.

For instance, you could set a simple action button labeled "Mark as Completed" to update a task's status in just one tap. My own early attempts taught me that small automations boost efficiency while impressing your users with how smoothly the app flows.

TESTING ON DIFFERENT DEVICES

One of my aha moments was realizing how critical it is to test apps on various screen sizes. In the past, I'd only look at the app in the Editor's emulator and assume everything was fine. But users will open your app on phones, tablets, and desktops, each with unique interface constraints.

AppSheet's built-in preview lets you toggle between these modes, so take advantage of that before sharing your app with others. It's much easier to address layout quirks early on rather than after users point them out.

REFINING YOUR INITIAL DESIGN

Once you see how the initial version behaves, you'll likely spot a few tweaks you'd like to make. Maybe you want a splash of color or a header image to give it personality.

Under the "UX" → "Brand" tab, you can select a theme, set an app logo, and even pick highlight colors. A little bit of visual flair can turn a plain list of tasks into something that feels polished and intentional.

I often emphasize having a clean design that doesn't overwhelm users. You can start small—adjust fonts, hide unused views, or add helpful icons to guide people. Gradually refine your style as you gather feedback and get comfortable with the Editor's capabilities.

SECURING YOUR FIRST APP

No app is complete without at least a basic security setup. While you might not need airtight corporate security for a small to-do list, it's still wise to control who can view or edit your data. In AppSheet, you can toggle between different access modes or require sign-in through your cloud service provider.

Don't worry about constructing next-level security at this stage. A simple sign-in requirement for editing privileges might be enough to keep things manageable. Once your app is more sophisticated or holds sensitive information, consider advanced security features like row-level filters and role-based permissions.

SHARING AND GATHERING FEEDBACK

Nothing beats real-world testing. Before declaring your first app complete, share it with a few friends or colleagues. AppSheet lets you invite users via their email addresses, and from there, they can access your app on web or mobile. Invite them to try adding records, adjusting settings, and even making suggestions.

I learned early on that user feedback is priceless—people will spot confusing field labels or request a feature you never thought of. Embracing suggestions at this stage not only improves your app but also builds user confidence. After all, it's far more rewarding to release an app that truly incorporates the feedback of those who'll be relying on it.

CELEBRATING YOUR FIRST MILESTONE

By the time you reach this point, you have gone from spreadsheet to a functioning, user-friendly app—a massive stride. I still remember the pride I felt when my initial prototype worked without errors and people actually enjoyed using it. This sense of accomplishment will fuel your enthusiasm as you continue learning more advanced AppSheet features in the coming chapters.

Building your first app is more than just a quick victory; it's the foundation of your future expertise. The steps you've taken—planning data, creating an initial layout, configuring behaviors, testing on multiple devices, and inviting feedback—create a roadmap you can follow for any new project. Each subsequent app will be smoother to develop because you've mastered these fundamental steps.

Congratulations on reaching this milestone. Now, take a moment to appreciate how far you've come. In the following chapters, we'll build upon this initial success, refining our skills and exploring new horizons within Google AppSheet. Get ready for a deeper dive into the world of no-code efficiency!

Chapter 5: Data Sources and Spreadsheets

UNDERSTANDING THE POWER OF DATA IN APPSHEET

Welcome to this chapter, I remember the moment it truly clicked for me that data is the core lifeblood of any AppSheet project. My first few attempts at building apps made me realize that if my data was messy or disorganized, the application itself would reflect that. From a simple spreadsheet tracking library books to more complex sources that integrated inventory lists, every app I created hinged on the quality and structure of its data.

In this chapter, we'll delve into **data sources**—where and how to store your information to ensure that your AppSheet app performs at its best. We'll also look closely at spreadsheets, which many of us rely on as our primary way to store and manage data. After all, a well-structured spreadsheet often becomes the foundation that allows you to build applications that are stable, scalable, and easy to maintain.

COMMON DATA SOURCES FOR APPSHEET

One of AppSheet's strengths is its ability to connect to various data repositories beyond all-purpose spreadsheets. While Google Sheets might be the first option you explore, don't forget that you can also integrate with the likes of Microsoft Excel, SQL databases, and cloud file storage platforms. Each choice has unique benefits:

- **Google Sheets:** Perfect for smaller projects, easy collaboration, real-time updates.
- **Excel Files:** Ideal if your team is entrenched in Microsoft's ecosystem, with robust data functions.
- **SQL Databases:** Offers higher scalability and can handle large datasets more efficiently.
- **Cloud Storage Services:** Dropbox or Box can store CSV files or spreadsheets for rapid proof-of-concept work.

My main takeaway: The data source you choose should match your project's complexity, number of users, and your comfort level managing that data. If you're just starting, don't hesitate to keep it simple with a single spreadsheet until you feel the need to diversify.

ORGANIZING YOUR SPREADSHEETS

Spreadsheets are the most common data source in AppSheet, especially when you're beginning. Although you can jump in with a table full of rows and columns, familiarizing yourself with a few **organizational best practices** saves headaches down the road. For instance, giving each table a clear, concise name helps when you're juggling multiple sheets. I often name them after the specific data they hold, like "Inventory," "Orders," or "Projects." This makes it crystal clear for both me and my collaborators what each sheet represents.

Another lesson I learned early is to maintain consistency in column headers and data types. If you have a "Date" column, make sure every row contains only date-format entries. This way, AppSheet can auto-detect the column type and create forms accordingly, reducing manual adjustments for you later.

WORKING WITH MULTIPLE TABS

One of my favorite spreadsheet tips is splitting complex data into different tabs within the same file. For example, if you have a project management app, you could keep tasks on one tab, team members on another, and reference data—like status or priority lists—on a third tab. Strewing all this across a single sheet can lead to clutter, but tabbing out your data categories makes everything more organized.

AppSheet recognizes these tabs as separate *tables*, allowing you to set up references between them. If you structure it thoughtfully, you can create robust relationships in your app without needing a formal relational database. This approach is often enough for mid-sized apps that don't require complex joins or massive amounts of data.

CONNECTING APPSHEET TO YOUR SPREADSHEET

After you've set up your spreadsheet, connecting it to AppSheet is typically a breeze. You choose your file from Google Drive (or another service), and AppSheet automatically imports it as a data source. The platform inspects each tab, identifies column headers, and makes an educated guess about field types (like text, date, number). While it's impressively accurate, you may want to fine-tune these assignments in the "Data" section to ensure everything behaves as intended.

Pro tip: If you rename columns or add new ones in your spreadsheet later, remember to regenerate your table structure in AppSheet so it stays in sync. Otherwise, your app might show errors or fail to capture new data columns.

SAFEGUARDING YOUR DATA QUALITY

No matter where your data resides, taking steps to keep it accurate and consistent is essential. I learned this the hard way when a shared spreadsheet got messy with duplicate rows and mismatched data types. Suddenly, my app's reporting became unreliable. Here's what I do now to keep things tidy:

- **Validation Rules:** Use AppSheet's "Validity" settings (e.g., requiring certain columns to be filled) to prevent incomplete records.
- **Filters & Slices:** Create slices to display only the data you need in a given view. This rule-based approach keeps your main tables uncluttered.
- **Formulas & Conditional Formatting:** Spreadsheets often have powerful built-in features for noticing irregularities. Use them to highlight questionable data before it even enters your app.

By implementing these checks, you ensure that the data feeding your app remains consistent and meaningful. This not only streamlines your workflows but also builds trust with your users—they'll come to rely on the accuracy and thoroughness of what you present.

EXPANDING TO EXTERNAL DATA SOURCES

As your app evolves, you might outgrow a single spreadsheet. For instance, you may need to reference a customer database hosted elsewhere or integrate with a web API that returns JSON data. Although these scenarios sound more advanced, AppSheet can handle them via its many connectors and integrations. You can combine multiple data sources into one app, pulling in cloud-hosted content, database tables, or even public data sets.

My own milestone was connecting my spreadsheet-based catalog to a SQL table that stored bulk order data. This let me see both real-time sales and projected inventory from two different sources—all within a single AppSheet dashboard. It felt like moving from a bicycle to a sports car when it came to data management capabilities.

MAINTAINING A SUSTAINABLE DATA FLOW

Once you funnel multiple sources into your app, you need a game plan for how you'll manage ongoing changes and expansions. If you're working alone, it might be as simple as scheduling regular backups of your spreadsheets. But in a team environment, consider designating data stewards who ensure that each table stays clean and relevant. Implementing version control on vital spreadsheets and restricting edit access to certain columns can also guard against unwanted modifications.

Remember, your data strategy doesn't have to be complicated from day one—start basic, then build guardrails as your app grows larger or more critical. The key is to remain proactive about data hygiene so you can continue delivering a reliable, seamless experience for your users.

ELEVATING YOUR APPS THROUGH DATA MASTERY

Drawing from my experiences, I can't emphasize enough how mastering your data source elevates your entire AppSheet journey. When your data is well organized—be it in a single spreadsheet tab or a network of interconnected tables—you give yourself the best chance at building an app that's not only efficient but also enjoyable to maintain. Users appreciate smooth, intuitive experiences, which often stem from a carefully planned data structure underneath the hood.

In the next chapter, we'll expand on the idea of data architecture by diving into *designing data structures*. You'll learn how to build on the fundamentals we discussed here, ensuring your app remains flexible, future-proof, and ready to tackle new challenges. Until then, take some time to reflect on how your data is shaping your AppSheet solutions—and remember that a solid data foundation can make all the difference.

Chapter 6: Designing Data Structures

EMBRACING A STRATEGIC APPROACH TO DATA

Welcome to this chapter, I recall the moment I realized that constructing well-planned data structures was the secret ingredient to making my local inventory app both efficient and easy to manage. Early on, I treated tables more like casual lists, but soon saw how purposeful data design could reduce errors, speed up performance, and simplify user interactions.

In this chapter, we'll explore how to purposefully shape your app's underlying data. A methodical approach—complete with proper naming conventions and thoughtfully chosen columns—opens up a world of flexibility as you scale to more intricate uses. Whether you aim to store details for a small membership directory or connect multiple complex sheets for a sales workflow, the strategies here will keep your data architecture robust and forward-looking.

ESTABLISHING CLEAR NAMING CONVENTIONS

One of my first lessons was that **consistent naming** makes everything easier to find and maintain. While it might be tempting to use short, cryptic column headers, meaningful labels will help you and your collaborators immediately recognize what each field represents. For instance, instead of "ItemID," consider "Product_ID," or instead of "Qty," try "Quantity_On_Hand." The key is clarity—anyone stepping into your data should be able to comprehend each column's purpose without guesswork.

Tip: If you find yourself repeating certain naming patterns, consider adopting a prefix or suffix system. For example, "User_Email," "User_Role," etc. This consistency will make your data table look seamless in AppSheet's Editor.

CHOOSING THE RIGHT DATA TYPES

Once you have your columns labeled effectively, focus on picking data types that align with intended usage. While it's possible to store everything as text, leveraging specialized formats—like Date, DateTime, Number, Enum—gives you precise control over how users interact with different fields. AppSheet's automatic type detection can help, but manually confirming each column's type avoids mismatches that might cause faulty logic or unexpected behavior.

- **Text Columns:** Ideal for names and descriptions.
- **Date/DateTime:** Keeps schedules and timelines fully accurate.
- **Enum or EnumList:** Constrains user input to predefined options.

STRUCTURING FOR RELATIONSHIPS

AppSheet shines when it comes to linking different sets of information. If your app tracks sales orders, for example, you might have one table for products and another for customers. Designing these as separate but *connected* entities allows you to reference customer details within orders, ensuring you never have to type the same data twice.

My favorite technique is creating columns that serve as references to another table. By assigning one table's unique key as the "Ref" in another table, you build a robust relationship that AppSheet can display elegantly. This not only speeds up data entry—by letting users pick from ready-made lists—but also preserves data integrity since everything is tied to a corresponding record.

KEY COLUMNS AND PRIMARY IDENTIFIERS

A cornerstone of good data design is the presence of a **unique key** column. This might sound obvious, but ensuring each row in your table has a dependable, unchanging ID can save you a lot of trouble down the road. AppSheet can generate IDs automatically, or you can manage your own system if you prefer. The critical point is consistency: as long as you never repeat an ID, your references and relationships stay solid.

I've learned that having an explicit key column also simplifies tasks like merging duplicates, restoring backups, or analyzing trends in external tools. When each record has a distinct identity, it's far less likely you'll confuse two similar entries.

PLANNING FOR SCALABILITY

Envisioning the future of your app's data is about balancing short-term needs with potential growth. You may start with a single table for orders, but it doesn't hurt to carve out a separate table for order statuses if you anticipate new status categories later. The same logic applies to user roles, payment methods, or contact details—you'll thank yourself when additions become a matter of updating one reference table, rather than restructuring your entire app.

A well-designed data structure also helps you minimize duplication. I've found it invaluable to identify potential overlaps between tables. For example, if you see repeated categories across different sheets, consider unifying them. This approach keeps the architecture lean and reduces the risk of misaligned data across sections.

MAKING USE OF VIRTUAL COLUMNS

For calculations or app-specific logic, **Virtual Columns** are a powerful feature. They don't reside in your underlying data source but live within AppSheet's ecosystem, derived through formulas or conditional expressions. I enjoy using these in situations where I want to display derived results without cluttering my base spreadsheets. It's an elegant way to enrich your structures while preserving the clarity of your core tables.

Example: If you have a "Subscription End Date" column, you could create a Virtual Column that calculates "Days Remaining." This keeps your main table free of extra fields, but still delivers real-time insights to users.

EMPLOYING SLICES FOR FOCUSED DATA

Slices act like custom views that filter or limit which rows and columns a user sees. If your app grows to hold large, diverse tables, slices help spotlight exactly what your users need. This also keeps the interface organized, as people won't scroll through unnecessary fields just to locate critical information. I've once built an admin-only slice to show private notes, while regular team members saw a slimmer version of the data without those extra fields.

The beauty is that slices pull from the same underlying structure, so your data remains consistent, yet you can tailor each slice for different tasks or user roles. It's a technique that offers big gains in usability and organizational clarity without needing to duplicate entire tables.

ADAPTING FOR ADVANCED USE CASES

Over time, your understanding of data design in AppSheet may spark ideas for more advanced setups—like partitioning data across multiple storage locations or implementing dynamic referencing rules. While these approaches are optional for small-scale apps, remaining open to them is wise if you anticipate scaling rapidly or integrating with external systems later on.

From custom status workflows to multi-table dashboards, robust data structures form the backbone of it all. Thinking through keys, references, and relationships now can save you from a messy rebuild in the future. And even if you only end up using a fraction of the advanced features, having a stable design pays off from day one.

BUILDING A LASTING FRAMEWORK

Deciding how to craft your data structures isn't just about short-term convenience—it's about establishing a reliable framework for anything your app might tackle. Whether you eventually add dashboards, advanced automation, or deeper security settings, a sturdy data foundation makes everything flow more smoothly. I've seen how a little foresight in table and column design can lead to apps that feel intuitive to end users and require far less maintenance over time.

Take a moment to review your own tables. Are your keys truly unique? Have you assigned descriptive names to each column? Can you spot opportunities to link data more efficiently with references or slices? By addressing these questions up front, you position your app for long-term success and reap the rewards of a well-thought-out data architecture.

Chapter 7: Working with Tables and Views

UNDERSTANDING TABLE ESSENTIALS IN APPSHEET

Welcome to this chapter, and one of my most eye-opening discoveries with Google AppSheet was realizing how much control we have over the tables that power our apps. Tables do more than just hold data—they form the central hub that shapes virtually every feature, from automated emails to filterable dashboards. When I first started, I thought a "table" was merely a place to store rows and columns, but AppSheet transforms those tables into dynamic elements that interact seamlessly with the rest of your app.

You can envision each table as a mini ecosystem: column definitions help keep data consistent, while references link it to other tables for a richer, interconnected experience. In practical terms, you might have one table for customer details, another for orders, and a third for feedback—then, AppSheet brings them all together in a smooth workflow. That's why setting up and fine-tuning your tables is such a pivotal part of building apps that are efficient, accurate, and enjoyable to use.

OPTIMIZING COLUMN STRUCTURES

Once you create a table in AppSheet (or import an existing spreadsheet), you'll see how each column is automatically assigned a data type. You can tweak these to ensure columns behave as expected. Maybe you have a column for delivery dates, which should always reflect a calendar date rather than a free-form text input. Setting it to "Date" in AppSheet means users get a neat date picker instead of typing errors that lead to messy data.

A personal practice I've adopted: whenever columns have limited, predictable values—such as product categories or shipping methods—I use Enum or Ref types. That way, people pick from a list or connect to a referenced table, preventing them from entering typos or invalid info. This small design choice goes a long way in ensuring data consistency across even the busiest apps.

CREATING AND CUSTOMIZING VIEWS

While your tables form the foundation, it's the **views** in AppSheet that shape how users interact with that data. Think of each view as a personalized lens that zooms in on the table (or slice) you want to showcase. Maybe you prefer a grid-like table for fast editing, or a simplified deck layout that emphasizes visual elements like product images or account avatars. AppSheet offers different view types—like Table, Deck, Gallery, Map, Calendar, and more—to suit various use cases.

In my early days, I stuck to the default table view because it felt familiar. But when I discovered the deck and gallery views, I realized how intuitive they could be for certain workflows. A card-like approach can be perfect for an app that displays a collection of photos or short descriptions. The ability to choose and toggle these views on the fly means you're never locked into a single design. As your app evolves, you can experiment with different layouts until you land on the best user experience.

REFINING DISPLAY OPTIONS

One of the most exciting moments for me was exploring the "Display" settings that let you tailor each view's name, icon, and position in your app's navigation. By customizing these elements, you help users know exactly what each view is for at a glance. For instance, if you have a "Dashboard" view that aggregates multiple tables, pick an icon representing analytics or charts. If you're displaying an "Inventory" table, choose a label that clearly sets it apart from a "Sales" table.

These small adjustments might seem cosmetic, but they create a sense of familiarity. Users can quickly find the data they need without guesswork. Plus, a well-labeled set of views keeps your app's layout looking sharp and thoughtfully organized.

LAYERING SLICES FOR TARGETED VIEWS

Sometimes you don't want to show the entire table to every user. That's where **slices** come in handy. You can think of a slice as a filter that narrows down which rows and columns appear. Then you can assign a view to that slice, effectively giving you a customized "mini-table." It might only show unfulfilled orders, tasks due this week, or leads assigned to a particular team member.

Using slices can be a game changer in more complex apps because they let you highlight what's most important for each role or scenario. In my own workflow, I tend to create separate slices for admin tasks, active clients, or archived data—each with their own dedicated views. That way, no one has to sift through rows of irrelevant records that only certain users should see.

CONFIGURING DETAIL AND FORM VIEWS

I still remember when detail and form views felt like a mystery. I'd see them pop up in my generated app, but I wasn't sure how best to shape them. Over time, I realized these views are some of the most powerful for user interactions:

- **Detail Views:** Show a single record's data in an easy-to-read format. Great for quick references.
- **Form Views:** Allow users to add or edit records, complete with input fields and placeholders that guide them through data entry.

By toggling through the "UX" settings, you can rearrange fields, add section headers, or even insert hint text to clarify what each field expects. This transforms a basic form into a user-friendly experience. Think of it like handing someone a structured paper form versus a blank sheet—they'll know exactly how to provide the right info.

ENHANCING VISIBILITY WITH CONDITIONAL FORMATTING

Once you have a view type you love, why not add **conditional formatting** or format rules? By setting conditions—for instance, highlighting overdue tasks in red text—you instantly convey which data points need the most attention. Whether you're marking a priority column or color-coding a status field, these subtle cues save time and reduce the risk of overlooked items. Personally, it was a turning point when I realized how a visual indicator could make it crystal clear which orders were behind schedule.

Quick Tip: Format rules can apply icons, text coloring, or background shading. Start with something simple—like placing a caution symbol next to a "High Priority" request— and see how it transforms your data presentation.

TESTING YOUR VIEWS ON MULTIPLE DEVICES

When you create or modify a view, it's important to test how it looks on different devices. It's tempting to trust what you see in the editor's emulator, but real phones and tablets can reveal spacing quirks, scroll issues, or font-sizing errors. I found this out when a table view that looked perfect on my laptop turned cluttered and cramped on my smartphone.

AppSheet's responsive design does much of the heavy lifting, but giving each view a personal test drive is still your best insurance. If something feels off, tweak settings like column width or font size. You can even create separate views specifically optimized for mobile. This extra step often earns appreciation from users, especially when they can comfortably interact with your app on the go.

COMBINING MULTIPLE VIEWS INTO DASHBOARDS

One of my personal breakthroughs came from discovering dashboard views. These specialized views let you display multiple data sources side by side, like a summary chart next to a filtered table. Setting up dashboards allows you to offer a high-level overview while still letting users click into detailed records. It's a fantastic way to create a control center for complex workflows—maybe an executive wants to see monthly sales, pending orders, and product inventories at a glance.

Dashboards are all about synergy. You can connect them to the same table or different ones, so users can quickly spot patterns or dive deeper if they see a spike in activity. This design approach elevates your app beyond data entry, turning it into a versatile business intelligence tool.

MAKING THE MOST OF TABLES AND VIEWS

In AppSheet, tables and views work hand in hand to deliver data in focused, visually appealing ways. When you define your tables to include clear column structures and complementary slices, you set the stage for polished, purposeful views. In turn, these views draw users in, empower them to filter or edit data easily, and guide them toward the insights they actually need.

Reflect for a moment: are there areas in your app that could benefit from a fresh view type or a strategic slice? Could a dash of conditional formatting make certain records stand out for better prioritization? Small tweaks to how you present data can leave a big impact on usability and overall data quality.

By honing your approach to tables and letting your creativity flow in designing views, you'll build an AppSheet experience that feels both professional and engaging. Your app will speak volumes through its layout and visual cues, offering clarity without sacrificing functionality. From this point on, we'll keep exploring the many layers of customizations and features that can make your app truly shine.

Chapter 8: Adding and Configuring UX Elements

ELEVATING YOUR APP THROUGH THOUGHTFUL DESIGN

Welcome to this chapter, I vividly recall the day I realized that user experience is often the dividing line between an app that people use begrudgingly and one they genuinely enjoy returning to. It's one thing to build a functional tool—tables, views, forms—but it's another experience entirely to weave in elements that look appealing and guide users effortlessly through each interaction. In this chapter, I'll share the methods and mindset that helped me craft UX elements in AppSheet that not only catch the eye but also create a sense of comfort and efficiency for anyone who opens my apps.

DEFINING APP THEMES AND COLORS

Selecting a consistent color theme was one of my earliest revelations in enhancing the look and feel of my app. AppSheet offers various themes by default, and you can even customize highlight colors to match a personal or corporate style. I remember experimenting with subtle blues for a calmer interface, then switching to bolder reds for a time-tracking app where urgency was key. Through these color choices, you can subtly communicate an app's purpose, whether it's meant to be friendly and casual or guiding users to act quickly on certain tasks.

Tip: If you're unsure which color scheme to pick, start with AppSheet's preset themes and observe how it feels in use. Gradually adjust color accents for buttons, text, and headers until everything aligns with the personality you envision for your app.

INCORPORATING IMPACTFUL ICONS

Another small tweak that packs a punch is integrating icons that fit each view or action within your interface. Let's say you have a view dedicated to project overviews—choosing an icon of a clipboard or a checklist can help your users instantly recognize where to go for crucial information. Icons also elevate the visual appeal, making your interface more intuitive. In my apps, I often pick icons that resonate with a universal understanding of the content. For instance, a shopping cart icon for "Orders" or a pin icon for location-based records. These subtle cues speed up navigation and add professional-level polish in just a few clicks.

LAYERING BUTTONS AND ACTION ELEMENTS

My favorite part of configuring UX in AppSheet involves placing and styling action buttons. These can trigger all sorts of behaviors—like adding a new record, sending out an email, or launching a detailed view of a specific item. Positioning them where your users naturally look can save repeated questions or user frustration. For forms, consider using a primary button within easy reach for quick submission, and maybe a secondary button to handle less frequent actions like archiving or flagging a record.

You'd be surprised how much a carefully placed "Add New" button can streamline overall workflow. When it's located in a spot that matches how someone's eyes scan the screen, users feel a sense of flow that keeps them coming back. And thanks to AppSheet's no-code philosophy, you can do all of this without getting lost in complex design tools.

DESIGNING CLEAR NAVIGATION BARS

Users often need to bounce between different parts of the app, so a thoughtful navigation bar can be transformative. I've tested minimal setups that feature only two main tabs—like "Tasks" and "Calendar"—when I wanted to keep things super focused. For apps with broader functionality, adding multiple tabs along the bottom or side can help categorize features. The key is to avoid overcrowding. Group related views under a single umbrella tab, and if necessary, use subviews or overlays to avoid a menu that's too busy.

From a branding standpoint, labeling each tab clearly with distinct icons serves as a visual signpost. If you sense a portion of your audience is uncertain about tapping a particular tab, try renaming it to make the tab's purpose crystal clear.

ADDING HEADERS AND SECTION BREAKS

Early on, I would cram everything into a single view, which led to clutter and user confusion. That's when I discovered how much cleaner the interface becomes with strategic use of section headers. If you're building a form that asks for dozens of inputs—like billing info, shipping details, and product specifications—segregating these into logical clusters can work wonders.

Consider adding a short, descriptive header above each cluster of fields. Bold text or a distinctive color helps users orient themselves quickly, and better organization often leads to fewer mistakes in data entry. It's a simple technique but one that can elevate the overall experience significantly.

EMBEDDING IMAGES AND MULTIMEDIA

Although not every app requires logos, photos, or videos, you might be surprised how often a relevant image enriches the interface. Maybe you run a parts-tracking system and want to display a product photo each time a user selects an item. Or perhaps you have a user directory where everyone likes to see friendly profile pictures. AppSheet enables these features with minimal setup: a dedicated image column can automatically appear as a thumbnail in a deck or gallery view.

My turning point: embedding quick tip videos for new users right in the app. It led to fewer questions about basic features and felt more personal. When used thoughtfully, images and multimedia elements bring warmth and clarity, giving your data more context.

STAYING CONSISTENT FOR A SEAMLESS EXPERIENCE

Consistency is a trait that I learned to value over time. If some views have bright colors while others are far more subdued, the result can be jarring. Similarly, an overloaded view next to an overly simplified one can confuse users about how to proceed. By adopting a set of core design decisions—like color palette, button shapes, and consistent labeling—you create a unified experience that feels familiar, even as users explore different parts of your app.

This consistency also makes future updates easier. You can roll out changes in style or branding more uniformly, sparing you from revisiting every single view to ensure it fits. The ripple effect is happier users, better engagement, and simpler maintenance.

REFINING THROUGH ITERATIVE FEEDBACK

Personally, whenever I finish adding or tweaking UX elements, I like to pause and let a small group of testers play with the new interface. Their gut reactions—like "This button's too small" or "It's hard to find the search bar at first glance"—offer a goldmine of insights. From there, I iterate, re-check the design in multiple device previews, and finalize once everything feels just right. This loop of implement, review, and refine allows me to ensure the UX is genuinely supportive and easy to navigate.

CRAFTING A USER EXPERIENCE THAT CLICKS

Ultimately, adding and configuring UX elements in AppSheet opens the door to apps that feel less like a spreadsheet on steroids and more like polished tools people enjoy using. With a few thoughtful adjustments—colors that match your message, icons that guide the way, well-placed action buttons, and coherent navigation—you transform your app into an engaging environment. I've seen how these little touches can turn casual users into enthusiastic advocates who value the work you've put into crafting a reliable, intuitive toolkit.

Embrace the creative side of AppSheet, experiment with new design elements, and don't shy away from testing different configurations. Each tweak you make—be it a vibrant header, an iconic menu tab, or a carefully curated form section—brings you one step closer to an app that resonates with its users. When all these details come together, you'll find that the line between form and function can blend beautifully, yielding a final product that's both powerful and user-friendly.

Chapter 9: Managing User Input and Forms

RECOGNIZING THE IMPORTANCE OF FORMS

Welcome to this chapter, I remember the revelation I felt after building my first forms in Google AppSheet. Until then, I imagined data collection as a simple matter of creating rows in a table. But forms turned out to be more than just a way to gather information—they became my primary channel for shaping the user's overall experience. By crafting prompts, defining constraints, and leading users through each question in a logical sequence, forms transformed the app from a simple data holder into a user-centric tool.

Forms are often the first and sometimes the only part of the app that users encounter. Whether they're entering personal profiles, uploading images for inventory, or simply updating a project status, the form design has a direct impact on how data is captured, validated, and organized. As a result, a well-thought-out form can make or break your app's success, influencing everything from user satisfaction to the quality of the data you receive.

TAILORING INPUT CONTROLS FOR EFFICIENCY

One of my favorite aspects of building forms in AppSheet is the ability to select from a variety of input controls—such as dropdown menus, toggles, date pickers, and barcode scanners. Choosing the right control not only helps direct users to provide the correct kind of data but also reduces errors and speeds up submissions. For instance, if you need users to choose from a fixed set of categories, a dropdown menu cuts down on confusion and typos. On the other hand, if you're dealing with inventory items or product codes, a barcode scanner can capture details in a snap.

Pro tip: Whenever possible, replace free-text fields with simpler selection tools to maintain clean, uniform data. This approach also keeps your forms feeling polished and professional, while greatly minimizing the chance for mis-typed entries.

UTILIZING VALIDATION RULES AND CONSTRAINTS

I vividly recall an early app that I created without any validation rules. I ended up with rows upon rows of inconsistent records, which made generating reports a nightmare. Once I discovered how to implement validation within AppSheet forms, everything changed. Whether it's imposing a character limit, restricting entries to numeric values, or requiring certain fields to be non-blank, these rules guarantee that every submission aligns with the data structure you've envisioned.

Beyond basic checks, you can set conditional constraints—like mandating an explanation if someone selects "Other" from a dropdown. These extra safeguards might seem minor, but they empower you to maintain reliable data integrity over time, even if your user base is large and dispersed.

STREAMLINING DATA ENTRY WITH PRE-FILLED FIELDS

One powerful strategy I use in my forms is pre-filled fields. By leveraging formulas and references, you can automatically generate default values based on prior user selections. Let's say a technician has already identified a piece of equipment for service—why not pre-populate the equipment ID and location fields, so they only fill in the details that differ?

Pre-filling transforms data entry from a chore to a smooth, guided process. In many cases, it makes sense to store a user's last selected values and prime the form with them the next time. This convenience not only saves time but also cuts down on repetitive mistakes, which I've learned can be invaluable for teams juggling multiple tasks at once.

CREATING CONVERSATIONAL USER JOURNEYS

When I redesigned an internal feedback form for a team project, I wanted to make it feel more like a quick conversation. By adding small section headers with short, friendly prompts like "Tell us about your experience" or "How can we improve?", I shifted the tone from formal to welcoming. That subtle tweak nudged people to be more open and thorough. In practice, you can do this kind of transformation by weaving in descriptive text elements or even dynamic show-if logic, so only the relevant prompts appear as users move through the form.

Idea: If you're building a support ticket form, consider stepping your users through "Describe the issue," "Name the device," and "Additional notes" instead of displaying all fields at once. This sequence feels more manageable, encouraging them to complete each step.

ENSURING ACCESSIBILITY AND CLARITY

One area many overlook is making sure that forms remain accessible across diverse user groups. Font size, color contrasts, and layout matter immensely for usability. AppSheet's form views are already responsive, but adding clear labels, placeholders, and validation messages can help all users, including those who might be less tech-savvy. If you notice certain fields generating repeated confusion, consider rewriting labels, adding instructional text, or clarifying the field's purpose somewhere within the form.

Clarity extends to the final submission step as well— offering a clear success message helps confirm that the user's input has been recorded. This small detail can reduce uncertainty and eliminate the urge for users to resubmit the same data multiple times.

TESTING AND ITERATING USER INPUT FLOWS

I find that forms must be tested just as carefully as any other app feature. It's easy to overlook how a subtle design choice might confuse a user. Try to place yourself in their shoes or, better yet, gather a small group to complete a typical workflow in your form. Watch closely where they hesitate or backtrack—these moments often highlight the need for improved labels, better input controls, or more accurate defaults.

After rolling out changes, keep your data logs in mind. If you see spikes in incomplete submissions or certain fields being left blank, it might be time for another adjustment. Forms are rarely perfect on the first go, but refining them doesn't have to be painful. AppSheet's real-time editing and previews let you iterate until everything feels just right.

BUILDING CONFIDENCE WITH USER FEEDBACK

Whether your app is a small personal organizer or part of a company-wide tool, managing user input can have a lasting influence on how people perceive your entire project. By smoothing out the form design, guiding data entry, and providing instant validation, you not only streamline the app's workflow but also convey professionalism and trustworthiness. I've had team members tell me they felt more confident entering data when the form's design was friendly and guided them through each step.

Ultimately, forms serve as the handshake between your data and your community of users. Every improvement you make—be it pre-filling fields, fine-tuning validations, or presenting prompts in a more conversational style—strengthens that handshake. The result is an app that consistently yields high-quality data while delivering an experience your users appreciate from start to finish.

Chapter 10: Incorporating App Formulas

WHY FORMULAS MATTER IN APPSHEET

Welcome to this chapter, I remember reaching the point in my AppSheet journey where formulas suddenly made everything "click." Until that moment, I viewed AppSheet mainly as a data-collection tool with neat user interfaces. But then I discovered how formulas could bring my apps to life—automatically calculating fields, displaying conditional results, and even creating dynamic workflows. In many ways, formulas are the secret weapon that turns a simple app into a sophisticated, problem-solving machine.

Incorporating formulas isn't just about making math easier. It can handle everything from text manipulations and date calculations to filtering data based on complex conditions. Whether you're creating a personal project tracker or a company-wide workflow, mastering formulas can help you save hours of time and elevate the entire user experience.

GETTING STARTED WITH BASIC EXPRESSIONS

One of the best things about AppSheet formulas is that you can start small. Suppose you want a quick property such as a "Total Price" field that multiplies unit price by quantity—just use an expression like *[Unit Price] * [Quantity]*. It's simple but instantly rewarding. Once you see that result appear in your form or view without writing a single line of traditional code, you'll realize the power at your fingertips.

Tip: Don't be shy about exploring the Expression Assistant in AppSheet. It's like having a built-in tutor that suggests possible functions, checks your syntax, and highlights any issues before you finalize your formula.

EMBRACING LOGICAL FUNCTIONS

Beyond arithmetic, logical functions let you tailor what appears or happens under specific conditions. A popular example is the *IF()* statement: **IF([Status] = "Pending", "Awaiting Approval", "Complete")**. This statement automatically updates a field's value based on an existing column's status. I've seen how this single formula can eliminate countless manual updates for project teams, ensuring their dashboards accurately reflect evolving statuses.

Whether you're designating certain fields as read-only for specific users or showing a warning message when an entry passes its due date, logical formulas empower you to sculpt the app's behavior with fine-grained control.

COMBINING DATA WITH TEXT FUNCTIONS

One of my earliest "aha" moments was realizing how text functions could automatically generate item descriptions, confirmations, or personalized messages. For instance, imagine a customer-facing app that delivers a friendly note each time someone completes a form. By combining fields like first name, order number, and date into a single message, you add a personable touch. A formula like:

CONCATENATE("Hello ", [First Name], "! Your order #", [Order ID], " is scheduled for ", [Delivery Date], ".")

…can transform a dull confirmation into something that feels tailor-made. This not only improves clarity but offers reassurance that your app is paying attention to the details that matter.

WORKING WITH DATE AND TIME FUNCTIONS

Dates and times can become messy quickly if you're not consistent. Luckily, AppSheet's *TODAY()*, *NOW()*, and *DATE()* functions simplify time-based calculations. You can track deadlines, measure how long a project has been active, or set reminders to follow up after a certain number of days. In my own experience, building a team schedule app using these functions allowed everyone to see which deadlines were right around the corner—and which ones were long overdue.

Quick tip: If you often deal with time zones, consider storing all data in a consistent format (like UTC) and adjusting only in display formulas. That approach keeps your data uniform behind the scenes while still giving local-friendly times to users.

FILTERING AND AGGREGATING DATA WITH SELECT

One of the first advanced formulas I experimented with was *SELECT()*. This function retrieves specific values from a table based on conditions. For example, if you want to grab a list of pending tasks assigned to a certain department, you could do something like:

SELECT(Tasks[Task ID], [Department] = "Marketing" AND [Status] = "Pending")

You can then feed this list into another formula—maybe to count tasks or display them on a specialized dashboard. The real magic happens when you stack logical operators. Before I realized this was possible, I spent hours creating extra tables or complicated views to achieve similar results. Now I lean heavily on SELECT to power everything from quick metrics to dynamic drop-downs.

MAKING THE MOST OF VIRTUAL COLUMNS

Virtual columns are a fantastic option if you want to display computed values without cluttering your underlying spreadsheet. For instance, I once needed a field showing "Days Until Deadline," calculated on the fly each time a record was viewed. Creating a virtual column with the expression *[Due Date] - TODAY()* kept the base data clean while offering a real-time counter. This blend of efficiency and flexibility is one of the biggest reasons I've come to rely on virtual columns so much in my more complex apps.

ENHANCING APP ACTIONS WITH FORMULAS

The interplay between formulas and actions can take your automation to the next level. Picture a button labeled "Mark Completed" that not only updates a [Status] column but also sets a [Completion Date] to *TODAY()* and sends a quick confirmation email. By embedding formulas directly into the button's behavior, you skip multiple steps and reduce manual oversight. It's a small addition, but these streamlined patterns can multiply as your app grows, saving significant time each day.

Idea: Link a formula to an action that calculates how many items remain in stock when an order is placed, automatically updating an "Inventory Balance" column. This live accuracy helps your app maintain real-time insights into inventory levels.

TESTING YOUR FORMULAS

Whenever you create or adjust a formula, it's wise to test thoroughly. In my early days, I remember forgetting to test a complicated *IF()* chain, only to discover half my data ended up miscategorized. Even small errors in syntax can lead to big headaches. Make use of the Expression Assistant to preview your logic with example data, and watch how your formula reacts to edge cases—like null values or unexpected inputs.

If something doesn't work as intended, try simplifying. Split a longer formula into smaller pieces, test each one, and combine them again once you're sure each part behaves properly. This step-by-step approach is easier than wrestling with a big expression all at once.

ELEVATING YOUR APP WITH FORMULA-DRIVEN INSIGHTS

Incorporating formulas has revolutionized how I design no-code apps. It adds a layer of real-time decision-making that fuels everything from small-scale reminders to enterprise-worthy automations. Whether you're generating custom text messages, calculating crucial metrics, or building interactive dashboards, formulas help you extend well beyond the basics of data collection.

By investing a little time in learning expressions and fine-tuning your logic, you'll find that AppSheet adapts to almost any challenge you throw at it. Formulas bridge the gap between static data and a truly dynamic user experience—an experience where the app not only records information but also thinks alongside you. That level of synergy transforms an ordinary project into something your users can rely on and return to with confidence.

Chapter 11: Enhancing Apps with Conditional Logic

UNLOCKING THE POWER OF CONDITIONAL LOGIC

Welcome to this chapter, I remember the moment when I realized how transformative conditional logic could be for my AppSheet creations. Initially, I was content just letting my app display static fields and forms. But once I discovered how to control visibility, enable or disable fields, and create dynamic workflows based on user input, the possibilities seemed endless. Conditional logic doesn't merely make your app smarter; it makes it more adaptive, allowing you to guide users to the information and actions that really matter.

DECIDING WHAT USERS SEE AND WHEN

One of the best ways to apply conditional logic is by controlling which UI elements appear under specific circumstances. By configuring show-if expressions, I can selectively display fields, images, or entire menus. For instance, if a user picks "Yes" for "Requires Approval," I might reveal an additional set of questions or a dedicated form. Otherwise, the screen remains clutter-free. This way, each user sees only what's relevant to their task, making the entire process more efficient.

Tip: When setting up show-if rules, try to keep your statements straightforward. If they start getting too complex, break them into smaller, easier-to-read expressions or consider using slices that filter data and simplify what's displayed.

VALIDATING DATA IN REAL TIME

Conditional logic isn't just about what's shown; it's also great for validating user input on the fly. If you want to ensure a certain field is completed only when another field is flagged, you can do that with an expression. For example, if a user selects a particular category in your form, you can make another field mandatory. During my early experiments, this allowed me to gently direct users toward providing the information I needed, rather than relying on trial and error. Over time, it drastically cut down on incomplete entries and saved me a ton of back-and-forth communication.

AUTOMATING STATE CHANGES

One of my most satisfying moments with conditional logic came when I automated state changes based on certain triggers. Let's say an employee checks an "Items Received" box—my app automatically updates the status column to "Received" and logs the date and time. This kind of behind-the-scenes logic keeps your data consistent without forcing users to manually update multiple fields. The look on my teammates' faces when they realized the app handled these extra actions was priceless.

Actions and workflows often go hand in hand with conditional logic. By pairing triggered events with clear rules, you can define sequences like "If stock falls below X, send notification to Y." It's a timesaving approach that boosts reliability for any process requiring multiple steps.

USING IF STATEMENTS AND BEYOND

IF statements are the cornerstone of conditional logic in AppSheet. With them, you can branch your application's behavior based on user input or existing data fields. Whether it's calculating a discount or directing none, or switching between two different form layouts, these expressions give your app a sense of adaptability. IF, combined with AND, OR, and NOT, can handle everything from simple checks to multi-criteria decisions. I've even discovered creative ways to chain conditions for more advanced scenarios, like auto-assigning tasks once certain boxes are checked.

Example: *IF([Priority] = "High", "Requires Immediate Attention", "Normal Queue")* can instantly sort critical items from everyday tasks.

DRIVING WORKFLOWS WITH CONDITIONAL BRANCHING

Whenever I need a customized user experience, I rely on conditional branching in workflows. For instance, a task might follow one path if a user belongs to a specific department or if a data threshold is crossed. Instead of creating separate apps for each variation, I let a single app determine which route to take. This is especially handy for organizations that require one cohesive workflow but have slightly different steps for different teams. By harnessing conditionals, everybody collaborates in one place, yet sees only the information that matters to them.

GUIDING NAVIGATION AND BUTTON ACTIONS

I recall featuring a "Proceed" button that only became active when crucial fields were filled. That simple change prevented half-finished submissions and improved data integrity. By tying the button's clickable state to a condition—often through expressions referencing required columns—I could ensure users followed a logical order. If you ever notice that users get confused about next steps or skip fields, enabling or disabling buttons with AppSheet's conditional logic can be a game-changer.

You can also automatically direct users to specific views based on input. For instance, if a person marks an order as "Urgent," you could navigate them immediately to a list of priority tasks, prompting them to either request expedited shipping or assign extra team members.

MAINTAINING DATA SECURITY AND ACCESS

Beyond enhancing the user interface, conditional logic plays a key role in safeguarding data. If you have different user roles—like managers, technicians, or interns—you can tailor what each role can see or edit. Conditional expressions can detect the current user's role and show or hide certain fields accordingly. For me, this proved essential when dealing with sensitive information, as it minimized the risk of accidental edits or unauthorized peeks into private records.

Note: While these expressions offer a convenient layer of protection, it's always good practice to reinforce data security at the table or slice level for truly critical information.

ITERATING YOUR CONDITIONAL LOGIC

The more I worked with conditional logic, the more I realized it's an iterative process. Sometimes you'll set up a rule and discover that users prefer a slightly different flow, or your business requirements evolve. My advice is to keep your logic flexible—organize your expressions in a clear, readable manner, and be ready to adapt them as feedback comes in. A small tweak, like adjusting a show-if statement, can create a big improvement in how your users experience the app.

You can also set up test columns or test user roles to explore new ideas without disturbing live data. In many cases, I've duplicated a table slice just to try out fresh conditional settings before rolling them into production. This extra step ensures that everything runs smoothly on launch day.

BRINGING YOUR APP TO LIFE

Conditional logic remains one of my favorite AppSheet features because it gives your creation that sense of responsiveness. The app "feels" alive, reacting to each user selection or data point with purposeful changes in the interface. This encourages a smoother workflow and empowers users to complete tasks accurately, all while guiding them to the right paths. When done well, your app appears to anticipate each user's next move, removing friction and boosting efficiency.

Ultimately, weaving conditional logic into your apps is like giving them a sense of awareness. From revealing additional form fields to automatically updating statuses, every piece of conditional logic shapes a more intelligent, user-friendly environment. It's also a skill that grows with you—once you grasp simple if-then-else statements, you can layer on more advanced expressions, create multi-branch workflows, and deliver an experience that feels fully tailored to each user's needs.

Chapter 12: Building References Between Tables

CONNECTING YOUR DATA FOR DEEPER INTERACTIONS

Welcome to this chapter, I remember feeling that spark of realization when I discovered that references in AppSheet were the real key to bringing my data together. Up until that point, I had been working with individual tables that existed independently. Suddenly, I saw how linking these tables with references could enable data to flow in both directions, making my apps more connected, powerful, and user-friendly. By setting up references, you can do everything from creating parent-child records to displaying lists of related entries—no extra coding needed.

WHY REFERENCES MATTER

When you build apps that handle multiple tables, it's rarely enough to treat each one as an island. In my own projects, I often had a "Projects" table and a "Tasks" table, and I wanted to link each task to its parent project. Without references, you'd have to copy and paste project identifiers into each row—cumbersome and prone to error. References solve this issue elegantly. Whenever a user creates a new task, AppSheet automatically knows which project it belongs to, and you can display all related tasks from a single project in one place.

Key benefit: Not only do references reduce redundant data entry, but they also lay the groundwork for dynamic features such as inline views and related lists that make your user's experience more seamless.

CREATING A COLUMN OF TYPE "REF"

To establish a relationship between two tables, start by creating a column of type **Ref** in the child table. Choose the parent table as the reference target. Let's say in your "Tasks" table, you create a column named *[Project ID]*, set it to "Ref," and point it to the "Projects" table. Now, every new task will include a reference to a particular project. It was an eye-opening moment for me when I first saw how AppSheet automatically fetched the name of the connected project, saving me from manually typing or validating the IDs.

My little trick: Give your *Ref* columns clear, descriptive names, like "Project_Ref" or "Parent_Project," so you remember the table relationship later on.

USING KEYS FOR STRONG RELATIONSHIPS

Behind the scenes, AppSheet connects these tables using each row's unique key. Think of it like a handshake—both sides must know which column holds the key so they can match records accurately. If you've set up a reliable key column in your parent table (for instance, "Project_ID" that's auto-generated), AppSheet will effortlessly form a robust link between parent and child records. When I first learned this, it made me more diligent about defining unique IDs in tables—no more partial duplicates or confusing references that break workflows.

Note: If you rename key columns or move them around, be sure to regenerate your data structure in AppSheet so these references stay in sync.

DISPLAYING RELATED LISTS AND INLINE VIEWS

One of the most exciting aspects of references is seeing how AppSheet automatically creates "Related" virtual columns. These columns gather child records tied to a parent, enabling you to present them as inline lists or embedded views. In my apps, for example, I show each project's related tasks right on the project's detail page. Users can click through and manage tasks without leaving the project view, which feels both efficient and intuitive.

You can customize how these related records display: choose a deck layout, table format, or even a gallery if you need a more visual approach (such as for photos or product thumbnails). This flexibility lets you tailor each section to match how people actually work with your data.

BUILDING HIERARCHICAL STRUCTURES

One of my biggest "aha" moments was realizing that references can be chained to form deeper hierarchies. Maybe you have a table for "Departments," which references "Divisions," which references "Companies." By nesting references, you enable a top-down navigation path that's easy to explore. End users can begin at the company level, view each division, and finally drill down to departments, all in a few taps.

This hierarchical design can also apply to scenarios like multi-tier approvals or item categories with subcategories. As long as you keep track of which table is the parent and which is the child, your references will handle the rest.

CUSTOMIZING AND BLOCKING UNWANTED REFERENCES

Sometimes you might not want automatic related lists to appear on every detail screen, especially if they're not relevant or might confuse users. In those cases, you can hide or disable certain virtual columns. I learned this technique when I managed a multi-table sales app and realized some employees got overwhelmed by too many related lists. Hiding non-critical references kept the interface cleaner while ensuring only the most critical relationships were visible.

Tip: You can also rename the "Related" virtual columns to be more descriptive, such as "Related Orders" or "Related Tickets," contributing to a more intuitive layout.

JOINING DATA FOR ENHANCED INSIGHTS

Once your references are in place, you can pull data from the parent table into your child records. For example, if you have a "Budget" field in the parent table, you can display or calculate it directly in the child table without duplicating data. This cross-table referencing had a big impact on my workflow—it turned my app into a hub for real-time data calculations. No more copying values into multiple spreadsheets or risking slip-ups caused by stale information.

Anytime you need to create consolidated summaries—like the total cost of tasks per project—AppSheet's references let you quickly roll up these numbers using formulas. The synergy of referencing parent fields and aggregating child records can give your app a powerful analytics edge, all without custom scripting.

PRACTICAL TIPS FOR MAINTAINING REFERENCES

Over time, I've gathered a few tips to keep references solid:

- **Ensure Unique Keys:** Consistent, reliable key columns prevent broken links and mismatched records.
- **Monitor Changes in Schema:** If you rename table columns or restructure your data, always regenerate in AppSheet to keep references up to date.
- **Consider Read-Only vs. Editable References:** Decide if child records should be adjusted by all users or remain locked to preserve data accuracy.

STRENGTHENING APP FUNCTIONALITY THROUGH RELATIONSHIPS

Building references between tables transforms your application from a basic data repository into a dynamic ecosystem of related information. This approach not only simplifies data entry but also guides users through meaningful paths—a sales team can shift seamlessly from viewing a client record to browsing that client's recent orders, or a technician can jump from listing an issue to referencing the relevant equipment's maintenance logs.

A well-planned reference strategy saves time, reduces errors, and provides clarity. You'll be able to craft views that mirror how your community of users naturally think about your data, making the app feel intuitive from day one.

Chapter 13: Automating Tasks with Workflows

UNDERSTANDING THE POTENTIAL OF AUTOMATED WORKFLOWS

Welcome to this chapter, I can still picture that moment when I realized my AppSheet apps could do more than just store data. I'd been manually sending emails, updating records, and juggling tasks—until I discovered how workflows can seamlessly automate these processes. With a few settings and simple expressions, AppSheet can spring into action whenever certain triggers occur, saving time and ensuring nothing falls through the cracks.

The beauty of workflows lies in their flexibility. Imagine you have a set of tasks that normally require repetitive manual work, such as confirming orders or notifying a manager when something needs attention. By setting up a workflow, you can let the app do this heavy lifting for you. That efficiency has been a game-changer in my own projects, reducing human error and providing real-time responsiveness.

SETTING UP BASIC TRIGGERS

Every automated routine starts with a trigger. In AppSheet, you might activate a workflow whenever new rows are added, old ones are updated, or certain conditions are met—like a status changing from "Draft" to "Approved." One of the first workflows I built notified a team lead by email each time someone submitted a project request. Before that, I'd rely on chat reminders or frantic phone calls to keep them in the loop. With this new automated approach, the entire process became smoother, and issues were flagged instantly.

Tip: Keep triggers specific. Instead of running a workflow on every row addition, specify conditions such as *[Priority] = "Critical"* to prevent clutter and focus on the most important scenarios.

DESIGNING CUSTOM ACTIONS

Workflows aren't limited to just sending emails or alerts; they can automatically carry out tailored actions. For instance, maybe the moment a request is approved, you want the app to log a timestamp, tag the request as "Active," and even update a related table. When I first realized I could group multiple actions into one workflow event, it felt like I'd discovered a secret productivity hack. Now, my app captures crucial data and keeps stakeholders informed—without me even lifting a finger.

You can also fine-tune each workflow step to suit your environment. Need an SMS notification instead of an email? Want to archive certain records in another system? The options are practically endless, especially when you integrate third-party services or use AppSheet's built-in capabilities.

BUILDING MULTI-STEP PROCESSES

I remember feeling slightly intimidated when I moved beyond one-step workflows to a chain of automated tasks. Let's say you run an internal approval pipeline. Once a form is submitted, you notify an approver; if they mark it "Accepted," another workflow sends an acknowledgement to the requestor and updates a review status. Although it sounds elaborate, setting up each step in AppSheet is quite straightforward—just specify the condition that triggers the next stage and choose the actions.

This chain can continue as far as you need. In my own use case, we had up to four layers of sign-off, and AppSheet handled each step. Not only did it reduce confusion about who was responsible for the request at each point, but it created a log of the entire process for auditing and reference.

RECEIVING NOTIFICATIONS AND ALERTS

While email notifications are common, workflows can send alerts via push notifications in the AppSheet app or integrate with chat tools for real-time messaging. For instance, I once configured a workflow that instantly pinged a Slack channel whenever a high-priority bug report was filed. Before that, critical issues could languish unnoticed in a spreadsheet for hours. Now, the moment something urgent appears in the database, the right people know about it, allowing them to respond faster than ever.

Pro tip: Balance frequency with necessity. An app that floods your team's inbox with dozens of messages a day can annoy more than assist. Restrict alerts to truly time-sensitive or important events.

MONITORING WORKFLOW EXECUTION

Nothing's worse than relying on an automation tool and later finding out it silently failed. That's why I always make a habit of reviewing AppSheet's workflow logs. These logs detail which workflows ran, when they completed, and whether they faced any problems. Early on, this practice rescued me a couple of times: once, a syntax error in my condition prevented emails from sending, and another time an outdated reference in a custom action caused updates to fail. Checking logs isn't glamorous, but it's vital for peace of mind.

It's equally important to test your workflows thoroughly before rolling them out to a large user base. Pop in some dummy data, verify the notifications arrive (or updates occur) as planned, and make sure the entire chain of events executes smoothly. Small adjustments, like rewording an email message or refining a trigger condition, can quickly elevate the user experience from mediocre to stellar.

SAFEGUARDING AGAINST OVER-AUTOMATION

One lesson I learned the hard way is not to go overboard with automations. There was a time I had so many overlapping workflows that a single data update triggered multiple email chains, each prompting different team members to respond. The app succeeded in making us hyper-aware of changes, but it also introduced confusion about who actually needed to take action.

If you find yourself drowning in a sea of notifications or conflicting updates, consider consolidating related events into one clean workflow, or let the user decide how often they want to be notified for specific tasks. Sometimes, giving people the flexibility to opt in or out of certain alerts is more effective than hard-coding numerous rules.

ELEVATING YOUR APP WITH SEAMLESS AUTOMATION

At its core, automating tasks with workflows is about enabling your app to handle mundane or complex processes without requiring constant input. Whether it's sending reminders, updating statuses, or chaining multiple steps, these automations free you to focus on what truly matters—making strategic decisions, crafting new features, or engaging users in more meaningful ways. In my experience, once you harness this power, you'll never look at routine tasks the same way again.

Reflect: Is there a recurring job in your current workflow that eats into your day? Could a well-placed trigger or a simple custom action take that burden off you or your team? Identifying these opportunities is the first stepping stone to building automations that genuinely enhance productivity.

By embracing workflows, you infuse your app with the capability to react, respond, and coordinate with minimal oversight. It's a step that can make your AppSheet project feel vibrant and proactive, gently nudging tasks forward with unwavering consistency. And as you refine your approach—testing carefully, checking logs, and adjusting triggers—you'll create a finely tuned system that supports users at every turn.

Chapter 14: Implementing Security and Data Governance

RECOGNIZING THE IMPORTANCE OF SECURE APPS

Welcome to this chapter, I remember the first time I shared an AppSheet app with a larger team. My initial excitement quickly turned into anxiety—what if someone unauthorized gained access to sensitive data? That experience taught me that app security and data governance aren't just afterthoughts; they're fundamental requirements for any serious project. In this chapter, we'll dive into the strategies and settings that help you protect your data, ensure compliance, and maintain robust oversight of who has access to what.

ESTABLISHING AUTHENTICATION ESSENTIALS

No matter how sophisticated your app is, allowing open or public access can lead to risks. That's why **authentication** is the cornerstone of protective measures in AppSheet. You can require users to sign in through platforms like Google,

Microsoft, or other supported providers. Doing so not only tracks which user enters your app but also allows you to tie data visibility and editing rights to specific identities.

Tip: For smaller teams, a simple sign-in requirement might suffice. But for more sensitive data—like financial records or personal information—consider combining authentication with row-level filtering so that even signed-in users see only what they're permitted to access.

LAYERING PERMISSIONS WITH ROLE-BASED ACCESS

Once you've established sign-in requirements, the next step is **role-based access**. I've found it especially helpful to differentiate between admins, editors, and read-only users. An admin might be able to approve new items and edit protected fields, while an editor can add or modify items but not change system settings. Read-only users can just view the data. By segmenting permissions this way, you ensure each individual only has the level of control they need—no more, no less.

In my own apps, I keep a reference table of allowed users and their designated roles. Then, relying on conditional logic and slices, I tailor which views, actions, and data each role can see. This extra granularity not only boosts security but also creates a user-friendly environment where people aren't overwhelmed by options irrelevant to their tasks.

IMPLEMENTING ROW-LEVEL SECURITY

One key lesson from my early experiences was discovering that not everyone should view all rows in a table. That's where row-level security comes into play. By filtering records based on conditions—like matching user emails or assigned departments—you limit exposure of sensitive data. For instance, if you have a table of employee records, only HR might see salary information, while department managers only see data for their direct team.

AppSheet makes it straightforward to set up these filters in slices or security filters. The difference is that **security filters** actually trim data at the source, ensuring that restricted info never even reaches a user's device. Whenever I manage confidential or legal information, I rely on security filters to minimize any chance of accidental leaks.

PROTECTING DATA IN TRANSIT AND AT REST

In an age where data breaches dominate headlines, knowing how your information flows is crucial. AppSheet uses **encryption in transit** when syncing data. This means information traveling between the app and the server is scrambled, preventing prying eyes from intercepting it. Still, it's wise to confirm that your underlying storage (like

Google Drive, OneDrive, or a database) also has robust encryption. Most cloud services offer *encryption at rest* by default, adding another barrier against unauthorized reads.

Reflect: When dealing with personally identifiable information or regulatory compliance, verify both AppSheet and your data storage provider meet the necessary security standards. This layered approach applies across all industries, from healthcare to finance.

AUDITING AND ACTIVITY TRACKING

I realized early on that logging user actions is just as essential as limiting what they can see. Activity tracking helps you confirm who accessed a record, what they changed, and when they changed it. AppSheet can log updates in an audit history, and combined with your spreadsheet's version history or database logs, you get a paper trail for troubleshooting unexpected changes.

Consider generating a custom activity log within your app. For instance, whenever someone modifies a critical field—like an order status or an employee's pay grade—AppSheet can automatically add an entry to a log table. This approach simplifies forensic analysis if questions arise about an edit or deletion. Plus, it fosters accountability by showing users that their actions are recorded for future reference.

BACKUP AND RECOVERY STRATEGIES

While AppSheet's real-time syncing is a tremendous asset, it's equally important to think about **backups**. I've learned to keep periodic copies of my underlying spreadsheets, databases, or other data sources. If my data storage is in Google Sheets, for example, I create weekly or monthly archives in a separate folder. This habit provides peace of mind in case of accidental deletions or data corruption.

Tip: Automate your backup process if possible. Cloud storage providers often have built-in versioning or backup tools, so leverage those features to schedule regular snapshots without manual intervention.

DATA GOVERNANCE: POLICIES AND GUIDELINES

Security isn't just about tools—it's also about having clear **policies** that every user abides by. When I first started building cross-team apps, I quickly noticed that people had different interpretations of "secure usage." Setting explicit guidelines—like limiting who can share the app, specifying data retention timelines, or defining how to report a security incident—keeps everyone on the same page.

Data governance also includes planning for compliance with regional regulations, such as GDPR. If you collect personal data from European users, you'll want to ensure that your app respects requests to delete data, obtains necessary consents, and logs transactions properly. In practice, this might mean adding disclaimers on form views or implementing a quick way to anonymize records once they're no longer needed.

DEALING WITH EXTERNAL INTEGRATIONS

One area that caught me off-guard was the number of external services AppSheet could tap into—like third-party APIs or personal cloud drives. Although integrations boost functionality, they also increase risk. Carefully review each connection to confirm it adheres to your security protocols. This might mean requiring unique, limited-scope API keys or ensuring that any data leaving your app is encrypted. Pay attention to the permissions you grant—accidentally giving a third-party service full edit access can lead to vulnerabilities.

By keeping these integrations specific and tightly scoped—only to the data they truly need—you preserve control and reduce the chance of exposing confidential info. This practice aligns well with the principle of least privilege: grant just enough permissions for the job at hand, but not an inch more.

MAINTAINING CONFIDENCE AND TRUST

Ultimately, implementing security and data governance in AppSheet isn't about locking everything down to a point of inconvenience; it's about finding the right balance between function and safety. Today, I feel more confident than ever sharing apps with colleagues and stakeholders because I know there's a solid security architecture under the hood. Plus, robust governance standards signal to everyone involved—from executives to the players on the front lines—that data is well-managed and treated with the seriousness it deserves.

Final thought: Continual monitoring and adaptation are vital. Threats evolve, and so do organizational needs. Keep revisiting your security settings, re-checking your governance policies, and stay alert for new features AppSheet introduces that enhance data protection.

By systematically addressing authentication, permissions, encryption, monitoring, backups, and regulations, you establish an app ecosystem that instills trust from day one. That trust underpins effective collaboration, ensuring everyone can confidently leverage the power of AppSheet without fear that critical data might slip into the wrong hands. With a bit of diligence, you'll have the peace of mind to focus on what truly excites you—building innovative, user-friendly solutions that transform how teams and organizations work.

Chapter 15: Deploying Your First Prototype

WHY DEPLOYMENT MATTERS

Welcome to this chapter, I remember the excitement of finally getting my app to a state where I was ready to see how it worked for real users instead of just in my personal testing. That leap from "in-development" to "shared with others" can feel both thrilling and nerve-wracking. When you deploy a prototype, you're taking your app from a concept that exists in your mind (and a few spreadsheets) to an actual tool that people can use. This transition tests not only the stability of your build but also how well it meets real-world needs.

CHOOSING THE RIGHT DEPLOYMENT MODE

AppSheet offers different ways to share your creation. For a basic rollout, you might invite a small circle—maybe colleagues, friends, or a pilot group of clients—to try it out. I found that starting modestly helps catch bugs before they appear at scale. More formal or larger rollouts may require a plan that coordinates user onboarding, training, and potentially advanced security features. Whichever approach you choose, understanding your audience and your objectives will help you decide how—and to whom—you hand out your prototype first.

PREPARING YOUR APP FOR TESTING

One step I never skip is running through a final checklist in the AppSheet Editor. Did I name my views and columns clearly? Are my core formulas working as expected? Are there placeholder entries in my tables that might confuse testers? Cleaning up small details beforehand maintains a level of professionalism. I also keep an eye on device compatibility by sampling the app on mobile phones, tablets, and desktop browsers to spot any layout quirks.

If you've been building and iterating for a while, you may have clutter—extra views or columns from old experiments. Consider tidying those up or stashing them in a hidden slice so testers focus only on the essential features. The goal is a purposeful, user-friendly environment so your prototype leaves a strong first impression.

INVITING A PILOT GROUP FOR FEEDBACK

In my early attempts at deploying prototypes, I learned the value of a dedicated pilot group. By selecting a handful of people who are open to trying new things (and comfortable giving candid feedback), you'll gather insights you may never have considered. AppSheet makes this process easy—just share the app with their email addresses and grant appropriate access levels. You can even create separate roles if, for example, you'd like a manager to see different data than a team member.

Tip: Encourage your testers to explore every nook and cranny. Ask them not only to add and edit records but also to click around intentionally looking for oddities. This level of thoroughness might reveal hidden bugs or user experience bottlenecks you wouldn't have discovered on your own.

REFINING APP PERFORMANCE

One aspect of deployment is monitoring how quickly your app loads and syncs. If testers complain of slowdowns, check the number of tables and the type of data you're loading each time. Perhaps you can move seldom-used information into a secondary slice so it's not fetched on every sync. Or consider employing filters so the app only retrieves relevant rows. Small adjustments in data handling can yield big improvements. After all, a speedy, responsive prototype does wonders for user satisfaction.

I also keep AppSheet's performance analyzer on my radar. This built-in tool highlights areas that might be slowing you down, such as large images, too many virtual columns, or complex expressions. By trimming or optimizing these elements, you enhance the overall user experience— particularly important if your audience spans various locations with different internet speeds.

COLLECTING AND IMPLEMENTING FEEDBACK

When your pilot group starts using the app in real scenarios, the feedback you receive can be surprising. Sometimes, a feature you thought was crystal-clear ends up confusing half the users. Other times, a tiny request—like adding a status filter—makes daily operations smoother for everyone. Rather than see these findings as setbacks, view them as invaluable data for fine-tuning your prototype.

In my own deployments, I often embed a simple feedback mechanism, maybe a link to a quick survey or a comments form. This makes it easy for testers to share their impressions without resorting to email chains. Once I gather and prioritize their suggestions, I jump back into the AppSheet Editor to refine my design, then push out an updated version. This cycle of deployment, feedback, and iteration is crucial for building an app that resonates with real users.

MANAGING VERSIONS AND UPDATES

After a few rounds of tweaks, you'll likely have multiple versions of your app floating around. One sign of progress is seeing how each new iteration resolves previous pain points. However, it's wise to maintain a record of what changed between versions so you can revert if major issues surface. AppSheet's version history aids in this, letting you identify which modifications might have introduced regressions.

Idea: Implement a small "What's New" section in your app notes whenever you roll out changes. That transparency helps testers (and future users) track improvements more easily and fosters continued engagement.

CONFIRMING YOUR PROTOTYPE'S UTILITY

Eventually, you'll notice your testers using the prototype more often or depending on it for daily tasks. You might see a spike in engaged users, consistent data entry, or fewer inquiries about how the app functions. That's a clear sign you've built something genuinely useful. At this point, you can start thinking about transitioning from "prototype" to a more formal release—expanding to a broader audience, introducing advanced security layers, or even integrating with enterprise systems if necessary.

Still, it's crucial not to rush. Double-check that your data structures, UX design, and back-end processes are stable. Deploying an unpolished app to a large group can create confusion and erode trust. The golden rule I picked up: if your pilot group is satisfied and you've resolved most recurring issues, then you're in solid shape for a larger deployment.

CELEBRATING AND MOVING FORWARD

Reaching deployment is a milestone worth celebrating! You've proven your capabilities to transform raw ideas into a tangible, interactive solution that others can appreciate. When your prototype is out in the world and receiving positive feedback, take a moment to acknowledge your progress. Reflect on the lessons you've learned—about data organization, user experience, and the entire no-code development process.

With your first prototype launched, you're better prepared for future enhancements or entirely new apps. Each deployment experience builds your confidence, expands your skillset, and opens your eyes to new features you might experiment with next. At the end of the day, the growth you achieve here is as important as the product you deliver, so be proud of how far you've come!

Chapter 16: App Performance Optimization

UNDERSTANDING THE NEED FOR SPEED

Welcome to this chapter, I remember those early days when my AppSheet projects worked great on paper, but slowed to a crawl once real data started pouring in. At first, I chalked it up to "that's just how apps behave," but soon realized there were specific ways to make AppSheet run more smoothly. In this chapter, I'll share the lessons I've learned about performance optimization—how to reduce sync times, streamline data calls, and build an app that stays responsive even as your user base and data grow.

REFINING DATA STRUCTURES FOR EFFICIENCY

One of the biggest breakthroughs for me was recognizing how much data structure affects speed. When you only have a handful of rows, things typically move quickly. But once you reach thousands of records or integrate multiple tables, unrefined structures can stunt performance. I've found it invaluable to keep row counts lean by archiving older records into separate tables or using security filters to limit how many rows actually sync to users' devices.

Tip: If you see certain tables growing fast, ask yourself whether all rows truly need to be synced. Often, you can define a slice or condition that only pulls in active or recent entries, lightening the load significantly.

OPTIMIZING SYNC TIMES

Early on, I'd get frustrated watching my app take several seconds—or even minutes—to update data. The root cause usually boiled down to how many tables I was syncing or how many calculations were running in the background. To tackle this, I started experimenting with the "Delayed Sync" feature, which allows changes to happen locally and then syncs them only when the user finishes. This makes the app feel snappier for people who just want to enter data and move on.

Quick strategy: Consider enabling the "Sync on Start" option only if necessary. If your data isn't hyper-sensitive, let the user manually trigger a sync. This approach prevents constant reloading and shortens the time it takes to open the app.

USING SLICES WISELY

Slices can do more than just filter data for specific views— they can greatly enhance performance by trimming down how much information is sent to each user. I discovered that if only one department needs to see certain records, creating a slice for them spares the rest of the organization from downloading data they'll never touch. Not only does this reduce sync times, but it keeps the interface clean.

Another overlooked benefit is that smaller data sets often help your device handle complex calculations faster. Look for slices that apply dynamic conditions (like "active tasks" or "recent entries") so you're not weighing down the app with outdated rows. Every second you shave off a sync can significantly improve overall user satisfaction.

MINIMIZING FORMULA OVERHEAD

One eye-opening experience for me was discovering how certain formulas—especially those in virtual columns—can ramp up processing time. If you have many virtual columns performing heavy calculations, your app can turn sluggish quickly. Instead, see if you can store critical data in regular columns or use spreadsheet-side functions if they don't need real-time updates.

When you do rely on virtual columns, try to keep the expressions straightforward. Nested IF or SELECT statements that reference multiple layers of data can be prime culprits for slowdown. By measuring the app's performance before and after removing or simplifying these expressions, it becomes easier to identify which formulas need to be trimmed.

LEVERAGING THE PERFORMANCE ANALYZER

AppSheet provides a built-in performance analyzer that breaks down each sync process. When I first ran this tool, I was surprised to see how certain operations—like loading images from the cloud or recalculating formulas—monopolized the bulk of sync time. The analyzer gives a visual timeline that pinpoints slow operations and highlights areas needing optimization. I quickly learned to run it regularly, especially after adding new tables or automation triggers.

Hint: Don't wait until users complain about sluggishness. Periodically check the performance analyzer as you build or update your app. Catching a performance bottleneck early saves a ton of effort later.

MANAGING IMAGES AND FILE ATTACHMENTS

When I started incorporating images and file uploads into my apps, I realized how quickly they balloon the data size. Large images in particular can bog down syncs, especially if multiple columns store them. Often, the best approach is to keep image resolution modest or store files asynchronously, so the main data sync remains efficient. Some teams even prefer hosting large files on a dedicated service and linking them back with a URL. This approach helps avoid transferring huge attachments each time someone opens the app.

Pro tip: If your app heavily relies on images, consider using a "preview" thumbnail column while storing the high-resolution file elsewhere. That way, users see enough to identify the file without loading full-sized attachments on every sync.

TESTING IN REAL-WORLD CONDITIONS

It's easy to optimize your app on a fast internet connection and think everything's perfect—until you learn some of your users have spotty Wi-Fi or data constraints. One of my big lessons was to test performance on various devices and networks. By simulating a slower 3G or poor LTE signal, I gained a realistic sense of how the app would behave for everyone, not just those in an office with fiber broadband. This kind of testing guided me to prioritize offline-friendly features, limit data calls, and refine large downloads.

Idea: Encourage your pilot group to try the app outside of ideal conditions—like a coffee shop with public Wi-Fi. Their feedback often reveals performance bottlenecks you'd never catch in a controlled environment.

ITERATING FOR CONTINUOUS IMPROVEMENT

Performance optimization is rarely a one-time fix. Every time you add a table, incorporate a new formula, or change your sync rules, re-assess the impact. I've adopted a habit of reviewing the app's performance logs monthly, looking for any new spikes in load time or memory usage. That routine check stops small inefficiencies from escalating into bigger headaches.

Involving your team or user base can help too. They're often the first to notice subtle slowdowns, especially if they rely on your app for everyday tasks. A simple feedback channel—whether it's a form or a chat group—lets you gather these observations fast, so you can act on them before friction mounts.

BUILDING A HIGH-SPEED FUTURE

Investing time in performance optimization might feel like an extra step, but it's one that consistently pays off. Every second you shave off sync times and every improvement you make in handling large data sets polishes the user experience and boosts overall adoption. In my journey, I've seen how a once-sluggish app can evolve into a nimble, dependable tool that coworkers and clients end up relying on daily.

Ultimately, performance isn't about chasing perfection—it's about finding that sweet spot where your app delivers the functionality users need without burdening them with long waits or clunky interfaces. By actively monitoring, iterating, and applying the tips we've covered here, you can build apps that maintain a responsive edge, even under rapid growth. And with each optimization you implement, you'll reassure your audience that AppSheet is more than capable of offering quick, seamless experiences, no matter how data-heavy the solution becomes.

Chapter 17: Customizing the User Experience

TAKING PERSONALIZATION TO THE NEXT LEVEL

Welcome to this chapter, I remember when I first started using Google AppSheet, I was thrilled by how quickly I could shape the interface with just a few clicks. Over time, though, I realized there was so much more I could do to align an app's look and feel with a company's brand or a user's personal preferences. In this chapter, we'll explore deeper levels of personalization—going beyond standard themes and icons to craft an experience that truly resonates with your audience.

Customizing the user experience is more than just picking a color scheme. From dynamic backgrounds and detailed branding touches to user-specific layout tweaks, every design choice sends a message about your app's purpose. If you're ready to deliver a polished solution that stands out, let's investigate the ways AppSheet empowers you to refine every inch of the user interface.

EXPRESSING BRAND IDENTITY

For many app creators, representing an organization's aesthetics is a priority. AppSheet lets you incorporate logos, define corporate color palettes, and even designate specialized highlight colors. If you consistently apply these elements across views, it helps users immediately sense that the app aligns with their company's identity. Sometimes, even small branding efforts—like adding a custom icon in the header—can elevate how polished your solution feels.

Suggestion: When assigning a primary color, make sure it has enough contrast against any text or icons you place on top. A vibrant but unreadable interface can end up confusing users, no matter how stylish it looks.

CUSTOMIZING NAVIGATION AND LAYOUT

One of my favorite ways to make an app feel unique is to customize its navigation flow. Beyond the default bottom or side menu, AppSheet offers ways to group related views or layer them within nested menus. For users who prefer minimal navigation, you can hide secondary features under a "More" tab—ideal for advanced functions that aren't frequently accessed.

- **Nested Menus:** Organize rarely used forms or views within nested submenus to keep the main interface clean.
- **Action Buttons as Navigation:** Place large, inviting buttons on the home screen or in a dashboard to guide users into the parts of the app most relevant to them.

By tailoring how people move between screens, you reduce cognitive load and make each user's path through the app more intuitive. This is particularly helpful when new users log in for the first time.

BUILDING PERSONALIZED DASHBOARDS

Imagine a scenario where each team member wants quick access to different metrics—a sales rep might want their monthly performance chart, while a support agent might track open tickets. AppSheet dashboards let you piece together these distinct data snippets into a single view. But you can take it further by displaying or hiding sections based on user role or preference.

For example, you can add a setting in their profile table that determines whether a user sees certain chart components. This approach transforms a generic dashboard into a custom control panel, ensuring that everyone sees exactly what they need—no superfluous or irrelevant visuals getting in the way.

EXPERIMENTING WITH ONBOARDING SEQUENCES

When people join your app for the first time, you have a golden opportunity to set the tone for their entire experience. Consider creating an onboarding sequence— several steps or screens that show them around and explain key features. In AppSheet, you can do this by adding additional views that appear initially and then become hidden once the user completes them. Adding short illustrations or well-placed text can help new users feel more confident right away.

Pro tip: Build a simple "Tutorial" slice with read-only data that highlights common tasks. This might include dummy records, clickable icons, or brief instructions. Once users grasp the fundamentals, the slice can automatically vanish from the main navigation.

INTEGRATING USER-SPECIFIC THEMES

While standard branding ensures consistency, sometimes you'll want to let individuals tweak aspects of the interface, like a light or dark mode toggle. By storing a user's preferred theme in a profile table, AppSheet can conditionally apply style features—maybe flipping background colors or changing accent hues based on a user's choice. This level of personal preference can be a game-changer for people who spend hours each day using your app.

You could also differentiate your interface for managers versus general staff. Imagine a manager logs in and the app highlights reports, advanced dashboards, or special actions in a bold color, while staff see simplified views in a calmer hue. By combining role detection with color and layout changes, you create an environment that feels tailored to each user's responsibilities.

ENHANCING FORMS WITH VISUAL CUES

I've discovered that even small form tweaks can transform data entry into a more engaging experience. Consider highlighting mandatory fields with a distinct border color or adding an icon next to them for extra clarity. You could also insert brief help text under complex fields, reducing confusion and support requests.

Another clever idea is using images or progress bars to indicate how far a user has gone in a multi-step form. AppSheet doesn't offer an out-of-the-box progress bar, but you can fake one with custom text or cleverly placed image slices that change based on the user's current step. This visual nudge helps them track their progress and stay motivated to finish.

INCORPORATING ANIMATIONS OR ENGAGING ELEMENTS

While AppSheet doesn't allow deep-level animations like a traditional front-end framework, you can still inject a little movement. For example, switching between multiple view types or showing/hiding elements based on user actions can mimic transitions that feel lively. Even a quick "Form Saved!" message that pops up and then disappears can temporarily focus attention, confirming that the user's action succeeded.

Idea: If you create a pseudo-progress animation using a sequence of views, each triggered by an action button, you'll give the illusion of stepping through a guided process. Subtle details like this can make users feel the app is actively guiding them rather than passively holding data.

SUPPORTING MULTIPLE LANGUAGES

If your user base spans across different regions or if you aim to make your app accessible globally, consider building in multi-language support. While AppSheet lacks a built-in translator, you can maintain a reference table of text strings for different languages, then reference them throughout your UX elements. By detecting a user's chosen language in their profile, you could surface the corresponding translations in views, menus, and field labels.

It takes some planning to manage all your language mappings, but the result is an app that feels at home in various cultural contexts. Whether you're supporting a bilingual office or connecting with international stakeholders, language customization shows you're willing to go the extra mile.

MEASURING USER SATISFACTION

Never underestimate feedback when refining the user experience. Even if everything looks perfect to you, actual users might find certain elements hard to navigate. Adding a straightforward rating system or feedback form in your app offers a wealth of insight. Ask brief, purposeful questions like "How easy was it to find what you needed?" or "Which features would you improve?" and let that feedback guide your next iteration.

As user satisfaction scores rise, you'll feel confident that your customizations are hitting the mark. Over time, these metrics become a roadmap for continuous enhancements, letting you zero in on what truly delights or confuses people.

CRAFTING AN APP THAT FEELS UNIQUELY YOURS

When you start weaving in branding, role-based layouts, onboarding sequences, and even multi-language capabilities, your AppSheet app becomes more than a data tool—it becomes an immersive experience. I've found that users are more willing to adopt an app when it feels thoughtfully designed with their needs in mind. By combining personalization techniques with intuitive navigation, the end result is a modern, user-centric environment that resonates with your audience.

The best part? These adjustments don't require a large design team or lines of custom code. Thoughtful planning and a few well-placed expressions can transform your app's entire personality. With each step toward personalization, you bring your users a sense of ownership and comfort—a perfect recipe for long-term engagement and satisfaction.

Chapter 18: Exploring Advanced Features and Integrations

BRANCHING OUT INTO NEW POSSIBILITIES

Welcome to this chapter, I recall the excitement I felt when I discovered all the advanced functionality that Google AppSheet has to offer. Up until that moment, I had been happily creating apps, refining data structures, and enhancing user experiences—yet I hadn't tapped into the broader ecosystem of integrations or specialized features that truly extend an app's reach. In this chapter, we'll journey beyond the basics and explore various ways to push AppSheet's capabilities further than you may have imagined.

By diving into advanced features, you'll see how to connect external systems, automate intricate tasks, and uncover tools that transform your app from a simple workflow utility into a dynamic hub that interacts with third-party services.

Whether you're aiming to link a CRM, sync inventory data, or harness specialized APIs, these expanded functionalities open new doors for creativity and efficiency.

UNLOCKING EXTERNAL APIS AND SERVICES

One of the most exciting frontiers is using AppSheet to communicate with external APIs. With the right setup, your apps aren't limited to reading data from spreadsheets—they can also exchange information with web services, retrieve results from specialized endpoints, or even trigger actions on other platforms. I discovered that once you master these external connections, you can build apps that schedule tasks, look up product details, or gather data from cloud-based tools you already rely on.

Tip: When integrating with APIs, make sure to plan authentication carefully. Some services rely on tokens or OAuth mechanisms, so confirm your settings in AppSheet's connector options to keep things secure.

EMBEDDING AND LINKING YOUR APP

As your AppSheet solutions expand, you might want to share data or embed interactive views in other websites or portals. Integrations like embeddable frames can bring specific portions of your app—like a dashboard or form—

directly into a company intranet or a public-facing webpage. Early on, I was amazed to see how embedding a filtered view into an internal site spared colleagues from swapping between multiple windows, streamlining their workflow considerably.

In addition, links generated by AppSheet can lead users straight to relevant app sections. For instance, you could email a custom URL prompting the recipient to open a particular form pre-filled with certain details. This approach makes it easier for people to jump in right where they need to act, instead of navigating the entire app manually.

INTEGRATING WITH THIRD-PARTY AUTOMATION PLATFORMS

A personal milestone for me was connecting AppSheet with other automation tools and services that orchestrate complex processes across multiple applications. By sending triggers from AppSheet into a workflow automation platform, you can chain events—such as updating project software, creating project tasks elsewhere, or generating documents programmatically. This deeper level of interaction not only spares you from double data entry, but also eliminates guesswork for your colleagues who need immediate updates in their preferred systems.

The driving force behind these integrations is the concept of passing relevant data from one system to another in a secure, structured way. So, if you find yourself updating many services any time a record is changed in AppSheet, exploring automation platforms can drastically reduce repetitive tasks.

TAKING ADVANTAGE OF ADVANCED UX CAPABILITIES

Beyond standard design features, AppSheet offers more intricate ways to shape your user interface. Think about using custom format rules that adapt how data appears based on time of day, user input, or external signals. During one of my builds, I configured color-coded progress bars that shift in real time as key metrics roll in from an external feed. Users instantly recognized what needed their attention, without diving into multiple views or generating manual reports.

Idea: Combine advanced UX tweaks with conditional logic, so when certain thresholds are met—like sales targets or event dates approaching—new elements or alerts pop up. This dynamic design approach keeps your app feeling current and user-focused.

SCRIPTING EXTENSIONS FOR ADDED CONTROL

For those who want more fine-grained control, you can incorporate scripting through supported extensions or hooks. While AppSheet prides itself on being largely no-code, there can be instances where a light sprinkling of script or a clever function transforms a user's experience. Suppose you need to run a complex algorithm or parse data in a unique format; a custom script may bridge the gap. In my case, I found this particularly handy for data conversions that app formulas didn't natively handle.

Note: When you venture into scripting, maintain a clear separation between no-code assets and any custom code. This structure helps you isolate potential issues if something doesn't behave as expected, making troubleshooting far simpler.

CONNECTING MULTIPLE DATA PLATFORMS

Over time, you might shift from solely using spreadsheets to storing information in an enterprise-grade database, or even multiple databases. AppSheet's advanced data connections can handle these scenarios by letting you pull from hybrid sources simultaneously. I once tackled a project that required reading product details from a Google Sheet while referencing an SQL database for bulk inventory stats. Thanks to AppSheet's flexible data connectors, syncing these sources felt surprisingly straightforward.

When designing a multi-source solution, plan for varying refresh intervals, user permissions, and potential synchronization conflicts. Ensuring that each data set remains consistent and accessible can be one of the biggest challenges—but also one of the most powerful capabilities—of an advanced AppSheet app.

REAL-TIME ALERTS AND CUSTOM NOTIFICATIONS

Another eye-opener for me was establishing real-time alerts that went beyond basic email or SMS. By merging your AppSheet workflows with specialized notification services, you can broadcast crucial updates to group channels, schedule daily digests, or even incorporate voice calls for urgent matters. This level of responsiveness fosters a sense of immediacy and transparency, allowing stakeholders to pivot strategies instantly when new data appears.

Some teams integrate chatbots that push AppSheet details to platform-specific channels whenever a trigger event fires. Whether it's sending a daily report or an automated alert about inventory levels, these messages ensure the right people stay informed—no manual updates necessary.

TIPS FOR BUILDING SUSTAINABLE INTEGRATIONS

Advanced features can significantly expand your app's scope, but it's crucial to design them thoughtfully so they remain stable. Below are a few suggestions that guided my approach:

- **Start Simple:** Experiment with one high-impact integration—maybe an external API—to gauge how it affects performance and usability before adding more.

- **Keep Documentation:** Record each integration's purpose, configuration details, and any keys or endpoints it uses. This practice avoids confusion when you make future updates or bring new teammates in.
- **Monitor Closely:** After launching an advanced feature, keep an eye on usage metrics, performance logs, and error reports to detect and resolve issues early.

PUSHING BOUNDARIES WITH CONFIDENCE

Embracing advanced features and external systems transforms AppSheet from a straightforward app builder to an orchestration platform connecting diverse data flows. It's a thrilling stage in your development journey—one where you realize just how much potential lies in a no-code environment when supplemented by well-structured integrations. Whether you're automating tasks across an entire department or creating custom workflows for a small startup, these tools offer a springboard for innovation.

My greatest takeaway: Don't be afraid to experiment. Each new connection or feature attempt, even if it doesn't pan out, helps you understand the ecosystem's limits and possibilities. Over time, you'll generate your own set of best practices, forging a path to sophisticated solutions that feel tailor-made for your organization's needs.

With this perspective in mind, think of each advanced feature you explore as a puzzle piece adding dimension to your project. Before you know it, you'll be weaving together intricate processes with a newfound confidence—leading to robust, user-centered applications that resonate beyond the confines of a single data source.

Chapter 19: Handling Updates and Version Control

EMBRACING CHANGE AND ITERATION

Welcome to this chapter, I remember when I first realized just how fast an AppSheet project can evolve. One day, you're adding a new view or adjusting a table, and before you know it, you're juggling multiple tweaks and features all at once. This organic growth is exciting, but it also opens the door to potential inconsistencies if you don't manage updates carefully. Establishing a solid approach to version control ensures that your app not only embraces new ideas but also remains stable and user-friendly through every iteration.

Many of my early AppSheet apps started off with simple functionality—just a few tables and forms. As user feedback flowed in, I added new features on the fly. That made sense initially, but once the app became a mission-critical tool, I quickly realized how essential it was to keep track of each change. Adopting a structured way to manage versions has since made it far easier for me to fine-tune, test, and even roll back if necessary.

LEVERAGING APPSHEET'S VERSION HISTORY

AppSheet provides a convenient version history feature that automatically logs each save you make to your app. When I first discovered this, it was a game-changer—I no longer had to remember every tweak I'd done or keep scattered notes in a separate file. Every time you click "Save," AppSheet records details of the update, making it simple to identify which version corrected that pesky bug or introduced a new data source.

Pro Tip: You can open the "Manage" section and check your past versions to see who made changes, as well as read short summaries. Adding clear notes each time you save is an easy habit to adopt and invaluable for quickly spotting when (and why) major adjustments were introduced.

MAINTAINING STABLE VERSIONS

Once you've created a few successful updates, it's wise to identify which version is your "stable" build. Think of it like a snapshot of your app at a trusted point in time. If you're making major changes—like restructuring tables or revising user roles—develop those on a separate "working" version while leaving the stable version intact. Then when you're ready, promote these tested changes up to your main deployment.

In my own workflow, I learned to treat the stable version as a safety net. If a newly introduced feature suddenly caused errors for my user base, I could revert back to the reliable build in just a few clicks. That sense of security encourages exploration without the fear of permanently disrupting a live application.

ROLLING BACK AND RECOVERING

About a year into my AppSheet experience, I made a sweeping update that reorganized nearly every feature—and it ended up causing confusion for half of my team. Luckily, rolling back to an earlier version was straightforward. AppSheet's version history let me temporarily revert the app to a time before the disruption. My users could continue their tasks while I refined the changes offline.

If you anticipate major rework, always verify that your last stable version is clearly labeled and easy to locate. It's also critical to confirm your data structure remains in sync if you've altered tables or slices—sometimes rolling back the app is only half the story if you've changed column names or references. Maintaining a backup of your data sources or using versioning within your spreadsheets (like Google Drive's built-in revision history) can rescue you in worst-case scenarios.

COORDINATING TEAM COLLABORATION

Working solo on an app is one scenario, but many of us eventually share development responsibilities with teammates. Having multiple people tweaking the same set of tables, columns, or formulas simultaneously can quickly get messy. That's where version control doubles as a teamwork strategy. By encouraging each collaborator to clearly note what they've changed, it reduces confusion and fosters a sense of shared accountability.

My practice: Create a short guidelines document or channel where everyone can post what they are about to modify. Even a single sentence like "Adjusting the 'Status' enum to include 'On-Hold'" keeps the group informed. Then, if something breaks, it's easier to retrace steps and figure out which version or change introduced the issue.

TESTING BEFORE DEPLOYMENT

One of the best ways to minimize errors is to have a "test drive" environment. Before you flip the switch on a new feature or significant redesign, share the test version with a small group of users. Let them poke around and try daily tasks to uncover any unexpected hiccups. Gathering that feedback up front saves you from frantically rolling back after you've already pushed changes to an entire organization.

When everything checks out, simply promote the tested version to your main branch. This approach keeps your production environment stable while giving you room to refine. And if something minor does slip through, you can quickly revert or patch it without entirely destabilizing the user experience.

COMMUNICATING CHANGES TO USERS

In my early days, I'd update an app and hope users would just "figure it out." Over time, I realized that providing a concise "What's New" note or a simple pop-up explaining changes boosted adoption and minimized confusion. AppSheet doesn't automatically produce a changelog for end users, so it's up to you to let people know what's different. A dedicated "Release Notes" view or a pinned dashboard message can serve this purpose well.

Whenever I'm rolling out a big shift—like a redesigned navigation menu—I'll also highlight the old versus new layout. This small courtesy saves countless user questions and helps folks adapt quickly. Transparency about your update schedule or upcoming features can even generate excitement and goodwill, rather than puzzlement or frustration.

INTEGRATING WITH EXTERNAL VERSION CONTROL

Although AppSheet's built-in system is enough for many projects, some teams—especially those with established DevOps processes—prefer pairing AppSheet with external version control tools like Git or enterprise scripts. While this demands extra setup, it's beneficial for highly regulated environments or large-scale apps with complex data structures. The principle is similar: store your app configuration, document each modification, and utilize branches or pull requests before merging changes into production.

Tip: If you choose this route, carefully maintain alignment between your external repository and AppSheet's internal version history. Regularly reconcile them to avoid divergence and confusion about which version is truly current.

ADOPTING A SUSTAINABLE UPDATE RHYTHM

Version control isn't just about technical logistics—it also guides you in establishing a healthy update rhythm. Perhaps you release minor improvements weekly and reserve major overhauls for monthly cycles. By defining a cadence, your users know what to expect, your testing procedures become more robust, and your version history remains neat and well-documented.

In my case, I found that dropping sporadic updates felt chaotic to my team. Instead, scheduling them in regular intervals helped everyone plan around system adjustments. It also gave me a buffer to gather feedback between releases and incorporate it systematically, rather than firefighting daily changes ad hoc.

SUSTAINING CONFIDENCE THROUGH CHANGE

At its core, version control is about building trust. It tells your users that even as you continually improve their app, you have a fallback plan if something goes awry. It shows your commitment to clarity—both in how the app evolves and in communicating any impacts on daily workflows. And for you as the creator, it delivers peace of mind, so you can innovate with fewer worries.

Once you've embraced a practical approach to updates and versioning, you gain a newfound freedom to explore. No feature is too risky or too bold to try, because you always have a stable foundation to return to. With each iteration, your app grows stronger, more refined, and increasingly aligned with user needs—an evolution made possible by thorough planning and a mindful approach to change.

Chapter 20: Effective Testing Strategies

WHY METICULOUS TESTING MATTERS

Welcome to this chapter, I remember how, in my earliest days of building apps with Google AppSheet, I'd feel a sense of triumph the moment I had a working prototype—only to discover unexpected hiccups later on. That experience showed me first-hand why *thorough testing* is more than just a final step: it's a pivotal process that can make or break everything you've built. No matter how small or complex your app is, proper testing saves time, protects your reputation, and ensures a smooth experience for those who rely on your work.

Testing isn't only about spotting obvious errors. It helps you unearth subtle issues in functionality, performance, user experience, and even security. If you think of your application as a story, then testing is your chance to proofread every chapter, guaranteeing that everything flows logically before readers (or end users) see it. With a structured approach, you can solve problems proactively and deliver an app that earns trust—both from your team and your audience at large.

DEVELOPING A PRACTICAL TEST PLAN

One of the most significant breakthroughs for me was learning to create a **test plan** before diving right into hands-on trials. This plan acts as a roadmap, clearly outlining the key areas you need to verify—like data integrity, navigation flow, and user access permissions. I've learned that every part of an app deserves a place on your checklist, from straightforward tasks like adding a record to edge cases like editing rows in offline mode.

My recommendation: Keep the test plan concise and easy to follow. List each feature (e.g., "Add new customer," "Sort tasks by priority"), state its expected behavior, then note any criteria that would reveal a bug—like incorrect calculations or missing fields. That clarity keeps your testing focused, so you don't waste hours repeating the same steps haphazardly.

BALANCING MANUAL AND AUTOMATED TESTING

When I was new to AppSheet, *all* my testing was manual; I'd click through forms, confirm data inputs, and try different path variations. Manual testing is great for capturing the user's viewpoint—how the app behaves in real-world situations. However, as your features multiply, you might find yourself running the same checks repeatedly, which is where **automation** comes in handy.

While AppSheet doesn't have an official automated testing framework, you can simulate it by using third-party tools that interact with web or mobile interfaces. In my own projects, I've merged these tools with the app's web version, scripting repetitive tasks like adding rows or validating forms under certain filters. This approach saves time and consistently checks core workflows after each update. However, I still maintain a lighter manual pass for tasks that require subjective judgment—like checking if the layout feels user-friendly on a small phone screen.

ENLISTING BETA TESTERS AND GATHERING FEEDBACK

One of my most memorable lessons came when I realized that internal testing alone wasn't enough. My perspective was shaped by how *I* understood the app, often missing how new users might interpret it differently. That's why inviting a small circle of beta users or a pilot group can be a game-changer. By giving them access to the app, you collect insights you'd never uncover on your own.

Encourage them to explore freely—opening views, updating records, trying advanced features. Some teams even run "live demos" where beta testers share their screens so you can see exactly where they pause or hesitate. This approach reveals usability hiccups, such as confusing labels, unclear instructions, or workflows that feel unintuitive.

COVERING EDGE CASES AND UNCOMMON SCENARIOS

It's easy to test your "normal" use cases—like a standard transaction or a typical data entry process—but real users often do the unexpected. They might leave critical fields blank, type letters in numeric fields, or try to reorder rows in ways you never planned for. Testing these **edge cases** prevents embarrassing crashes or confusing error messages.

Idea: Create a list of possible mishaps, like entering nonsensical values, logging in as an unauthorized role, or rapidly submitting forms multiple times. Throw these curveballs during your checks to see if your validations and error handling hold up.

TESTING ACROSS DEVICES AND ENVIRONMENTS

When I started seeing how different AppSheet apps looked on tablets versus phones, I understood the importance of *multi-device* testing. Some layouts that appear crisp on a large monitor might become cramped on a smaller screen, leading to layout shifts or hidden buttons. If your user base is diverse, consider that some might use Android, others iOS, and some will stick to desktops and laptops.

Be sure also to explore various network conditions. An app that runs perfectly on fast Wi-Fi can behave differently on a slower cellular connection. This is where testing offline and checking if your sync settings work as intended become essential. I remember watching one colleague struggle with a half-finished form in a rural area while the app tried to sync. Once I addressed those offline capabilities, the difference in usability was night and day.

TRACKING BUGS AND REFINING YOUR PROCESS

Discovering issues doesn't end at simply noting them down; how you manage and prioritize them matters just as much. When I first gathered bug reports, I dropped them haphazardly in a spreadsheet—only to lose track of some critical fixes. Now, I rely on a quick bug-tracking setup where each reported issue gets an ID, a brief description, and a status signifying whether it's pending, in-progress, or resolved.

Include a column for "Steps to Reproduce" so you can replicate the error precisely. Once you fix a bug, cycle back to test it thoroughly in similar conditions. This structured loop—detect, fix, retest—assures you really nailed the problem and didn't introduce new ones in the process. Then, move it to "closed" status and keep that record for reference, in case a similar issue pops up down the line.

STRIVING FOR CONTINUOUS IMPROVEMENT

Testing isn't a one-time event you do right before launch—it's an ongoing practice. Every time you add a feature or change a data workflow, you risk destabilizing some part of your app. Embracing **continuous testing** means baking small checks into every phase: from initial design, all the way to each minor update that hits production. It's more than just quality assurance; it's a mindset that values curiosity and thoroughness.

My personal rule: Whenever you tweak something major, run at least a short test pass. Confirm your new logic, ensure you didn't break existing features, and then proceed with a purposeful rollout. By remaining vigilant, you maintain an app that evolves steadily—without sacrificing reliability.

Effective testing strategies are an insurance policy for the innovations you bring to life in AppSheet. From mapping out a clear test plan and balancing manual versus automated checks to enlisting genuine user feedback and tackling edge cases, these methods bolster your app's resilience. Ultimately, each round of testing equips you with the confidence to iterate faster, adapt to changing requirements, and deliver a user experience that feels trustworthy and refined at every turn.

Chapter 21: Collaborating with Teams

EMBRACING COLLECTIVE APP BUILDING

Welcome to this chapter, I remember the excitement I felt when my boss invited me to co-develop an internal tool in AppSheet. Up to that point, I had been working solo, relying mostly on my own ideas and testing processes. But as soon as team members joined the project—some folks with data expertise, others with only a passing familiarity with spreadsheets—my approach to app-building had to evolve. Suddenly, collaboration became a central pillar of everything I did.

When you open the door to team-based development, you access a broader pool of creativity and knowledge, ensuring the end product addresses multiple viewpoints. In my experience, aligning everyone's styles and requirements can feel energizing but also challenging. That's why it's so important to plan your collaboration strategy from the start—defining roles, setting clear guidelines, and creating feedback loops. With the right setup, your AppSheet project can thrive on the synergy of many minds working in unison.

DEFINING ROLES AND RESPONSIBILITIES

One of the first steps in team collaboration is assigning **clear roles** within AppSheet. Some people might excel at organizing data structures, while others focus on UX design or automation. Giving each contributor a responsibility that matches their strengths helps everyone remain engaged and speeds up app development. In past projects, we assigned data-savvy teammates as "Column Curators," ensuring that columns were consistent and aligned with business needs, while our design-oriented members took charge of customizing the views and overall aesthetics.

Tip: If you have a larger group, consider a short "kickoff" meeting. During that call, clarify each person's domain— like who manages data rules, who handles user interface adjustments, and who oversees future feature requests. This clarity lowers the risk of duplicating efforts or stepping on each other's toes.

COORDINATING IN REAL-TIME

When multiple people edit the same app at once, it's essential to establish **real-time collaboration guidelines**. AppSheet automatically merges changes under the hood, but confusion can arise if two team members simultaneously rename columns or rearrange views. I discovered that setting "edit windows" for different components helped us avoid chaos. For instance, we might block off Tuesday afternoons to tackle data structure updates, while an evening slot was reserved for adjusting the UX layout.

Idea: Use a shared spreadsheet or a messaging channel specifically for logging planned changes. Even a quick note like "Adjusting columns for Inventory table this Wednesday" prevents others from making conflicting adjustments at the same time.

REVIEWING CHANGES BEFORE PUBLISHING

Deploying partial or untested modifications can disrupt an entire team's workflow. To safeguard against this, I recommend using **test versions** or "dev branches" of your app. Teammates can test their tweaks privately, confirm everything works smoothly, and only then merge changes into the main version. This approach is particularly handy when introducing larger features or reorganizing multiple tables.

Another strategy I've used is a simple "peer review" system. Before finalizing a UI switch or workflow automation, a second team member previews and tests it. That minimal gatekeeping step has saved us countless hours fixing avoidable errors. It also encourages knowledge sharing— since each contributor gains insight into others' specialized tasks, from table configurations to advanced logic.

SHARING FEEDBACK EFFICIENTLY

Collaboration shines when everyone's perspective is heard. But I recall times when feedback trickled in through random emails or passing hallway conversations, and crucial suggestions got lost. Eventually, we switched to a central channel (like a group chat or a dedicated feedback form within the app) to consolidate all commentary. That way, we could track and address each point systematically.

In addition, consider scheduling periodic check-ins— maybe weekly or bi-weekly—to showcase progress and solicit focused feedback. In my team, short reviews helped us catch misalignments early. This steady loop of "build, review, refine" allows small adjustments before they balloon into bigger redesigns down the line.

COORDINATING USER PERMISSIONS AND SECURITY

With teamwork comes the challenge of **managing user privileges**. Some colleagues might be full co-authors, needing the ability to alter workflows; others might just need to observe or provide occasional input. You can address this by setting role-based permissions and leveraging AppSheet's secure sign-in controls. This ensures that only authorized users can modify the underlying data or push major updates.

When the app eventually goes live to the rest of your organization, it's helpful to regulate access carefully. Restricting certain views or features to specific roles helps prevent accidental edits and extends a sense of accountability to each participant. In practice, balancing openness with security fosters a trusted environment, where everyone understands they have precisely the privileges they need—no more, no less.

DOCUMENTING COLLABORATIVE BEST PRACTICES

One aha moment for me was realizing how quickly a well-structured knowledge base can unite a team. We kept a shared folder of mini-guides explaining our data conventions, naming standards, and typical UX patterns. This living document spared new contributors from sifting through old conversations or making blind guesses. They could simply flip through these references to see *why* we used certain approaches and how to adopt them consistently.

When your team grows or if turnover occurs, this documentation becomes invaluable. New members can adopt best practices from day one, while seasoned members have a reliable reference to ensure continuity. It's also a great place to capture lessons learned—like a formula approach that didn't work or a UI design that sparked confusion among early testers.

MAINTAINING ONGOING ALIGNMENT

Collaboration doesn't stop once the core features are built. Regularly sync up to decide what's next—maybe a new module, refined layout, or advanced workflow. I've found that checking in on your broader roadmap helps you stay agile. Because let's face it: business requirements shift, and new insights emerge after you see how real users interact with the app. Keeping a stance of adaptability allows your team to pivot and innovate without losing the cohesive thread that ties all your work together.

Quick suggestion: Every month or quarter, host a short retrospective meeting. Ask: "What's working well in our app? What's frustrating? Which new features should we prioritize?" This democratic approach motivates teammates to keep shaping the app's direction collectively.

CELEBRATING TEAM ACHIEVEMENTS

It's all too easy to focus on deadlines and deliverables, but I've learned the importance of recognizing small wins. Did a teammate fix a tricky bug? Finally perfect that new workflow? Or maybe they simplified the user interface based on pilot feedback. Celebrating these moments—whether through a quick group message or a mention in a meeting—boosts morale. It reminds everyone that this collaborative journey isn't just about tasks and sprints; it's also about forging a product that reflects a diverse set of talents and perspectives.

Eventually, your combined expertise results in an app that feels robust, well-thought-out, and representative of everybody's input. That sense of shared ownership builds excitement and loyalty toward the project, ensuring not only a smoother development process but also a more polished final outcome that users genuinely love.

Chapter 22: Scaling Your App for Growth

EMBRACING LARGER DEMANDS

Welcome to this chapter, I remember when my very first AppSheet project started out as a small departmental tool. Initially, just a handful of people used it—adding a few rows here, tweaking a form there. But as others caught on to its convenience, the user base expanded rapidly. Suddenly, questions of performance, data capacity, and broader adoption began to loom large. In this chapter, we'll explore the strategies for taking your AppSheet solution from a neat, localized project to a robust, widely adopted platform that gracefully handles bigger workloads and evolving demands.

RECOGNIZING SIGNS OF GROWTH

Before you start revamping everything, it helps to recognize when your app needs to scale in the first place. Often, this awareness comes from observing patterns like frequent sync delays, a spike in error reports, or new teams requesting access. You might also see your data structures balloon, with tables that were once concise now overflowing with thousands of rows. These signs signal that you've reached a juncture where scaling is no longer an option but a necessity.

Practical tip: Keep tabs on user feedback and performance metrics. If multiple people report sluggish load times and you notice your data set has quadrupled, you'll know it's time to evaluate your app's architecture for greater efficiency.

OPTIMIZING DATA ARCHITECTURE

One of the first steps toward smooth scalability is ensuring your data is structured for the long haul. Review each table and confirm that no single table is overloaded with irrelevant rows or columns. Where possible, **split large tables** into more manageable ones—especially if certain records become inactive or primarily belong to historical archives. You can then build relationships across these tables without requiring every sync to pull massive amounts of legacy information.

If your organization maintains external databases—like SQL or cloud-based warehouses—consider transitioning essential data there. AppSheet's direct connectors let you tap into these stores securely while still enjoying the no-code approach. By offloading storage and heavier queries to robust back-end systems, your app remains swift, even under heavy loads.

USING SLICES AND FILTERING TECHNIQUES

One of my lessons during an expansion phase was to rethink the all-inclusive approach of syncing every table to every user. Instead, use *slices* and *row filters* so each person only retrieves the data that matters to their role or project. Not only does this cut down on clutter in the interface, but it also trims sync times significantly.

When you know certain records are accessed only by specific departments, why force everyone else to download them? By crafting well-targeted slices and combining them with security filters, each user gets a focused subset of data that keeps load times short and helps your app remain snappy, even as the overall data set swells.

ENHANCING APP INFRASTRUCTURE

As user counts climb, infrastructure planning becomes more vital. If you're integrating third-party services—for instance, sending data to a CRM or receiving inputs from an external platform—make sure these pipelines can handle higher transaction volumes. Look into **rate limits** or **API quotas** that might throttle your connections. You don't want a surge in usage to trigger unexpected slowdowns or cutoffs.

Additionally, evaluate the subscription tier for your AppSheet account. Premium or enterprise plans often provide more robust usage allowances, advanced security features, and performance optimizations that cater to apps with extensive user bases. If your app is mission-critical, making that upgrade can offer both technical and organizational benefits, such as dedicated support and guaranteed service levels.

CREATING SCALABLE WORKFLOWS

My first real challenge with high-volume automation came when dozens of teammates triggered the same workflow throughout the day, causing near-constant activity. Although AppSheet manages concurrency well, complex workflows—like sending multiple emails, updating numerous records, or calling external APIs—can become bottlenecks if they fire nonstop. Consider grouping or scheduling your automations during non-peak hours, or simplifying them to reduce the number of steps.

An alternative is to consolidate smaller, repetitive tasks into broader, more efficient routines. For instance, rather than emailing a report each time someone logs a new entry, batch those notifications into a single digest. This approach dramatically cuts back on overhead while still keeping everyone informed.

ADAPTING TO MULTIPLE TEAMS AND LOCATIONS

When your user base expands across different geographical sites or departments, controlling feature access becomes essential. At some point, you may need to customize certain elements—like forms or language strings—for each region. Under these circumstances, *role-based slices* can provide the flexibility to show or hide specific features without duplicating the entire app.

Hint: Consider building a "master" app structure that addresses universal needs, then use slices, references, or localized views for specialized requirements. It strikes a balance between a unified app and distinct regional or departmental features.

MONITORING USAGE AND PERFORMANCE METRICS

Scaling effectively depends on consistent performance monitoring. In my own experience, I discovered users from different time zones tended to sync data around the same hours, creating momentary spikes. By observing these patterns, you can predict and preempt slowdowns—for example, by adjusting workflow schedules or reinforcing your data architecture right before peak times.

Most importantly, solicit direct feedback from team leads and power users. Ask them if they frequently experience lag or encounter hiccups, then pair that anecdotal evidence with actual sync logs and performance analyzer reports. This combination sheds light on how real usage aligns with your app's design assumptions—and points you toward incremental or larger-scale fixes when data volumes soar.

PLANNING FOR CONTINUAL EVOLUTION

In the end, scaling an AppSheet solution isn't a one-and-done task. Your organization's goals, user needs, and data footprints will keep shifting. By staying proactive—surveying usage patterns, refining your architecture, and upgrading capabilities—you'll remain in a position of control rather than playing catch-up every time a new group wants to join or a new feature emerges.

I've seen how a well-scaled AppSheet app can become a cornerstone of daily operations, winning over entire departments. Users appreciate its responsiveness and robust feature set, and you'll be relieved to know it can gracefully handle the additional load. Put simply, a forward-thinking approach to scaling paves the way for sustained growth, letting your app—and your team—thrive in the long run.

Chapter 23: Troubleshooting Common Issues

RECOGNIZING THE EARLY SIGNS OF TROUBLE

Welcome to this chapter, I remember the first time I faced a puzzling error message in AppSheet. Everything had been running smoothly, but suddenly I got stuck, staring at a screen that simply wouldn't load. I know firsthand how frustrating it can be when an app that worked so well yesterday throws an unexpected tantrum. When something goes awry—whether it's a slow sync, a missing view, or an incorrect formula result—that's your signal to switch into troubleshooting mode. Recognizing the warning signs early on tilts the odds in your favor for a quick recovery.

Often, the first clues come from user complaints: someone can't log in, a form never finishes loading, or a column in a table displays erroneous data. I've found that paying attention to these early reports saves time. Rather than explaining issues away, I make it a priority to investigate immediately and gather as much context as possible. Below, we'll explore some of the most common pitfalls and how to tackle them step by step.

DIAGNOSING DATA DISCREPANCIES

One recurring snag I've encountered is data that doesn't show up the way you expect. Maybe a table fails to refresh, or certain rows appear blank. In these instances, the cause often lies in a mismatch between your spreadsheet and AppSheet's column definitions. Check whether a column got renamed (even subtly) or if its data type was modified without regenerating the structure. A quick sync or a manual "Regenerate Structure" can fix the mismatch.

Personal tip: Keep a habit of verifying column headers in your spreadsheet whenever you make a big change. A stray space or a slight re-label can lead to surprisingly tough-to-spot errors within your app.

HANDLING UNEXPECTED SYNC ERRORS

Few things cause more panic than a sync that stalls or fails altogether. Sometimes you'll notice a generic error like "Unable to fetch app definition" or "Sync error." These issues might stem from an unstable internet connection, disrupted data sources, or formula overload. My first step is always to confirm the app is online and my data source is operational—especially if it's a shared spreadsheet or a database requiring credentials.

If everything appears fine but the sync continues to fail, simplify your problem-solving. Temporarily disable or remove large slices, complex virtual columns, or advanced workflows. Then add them back one at a time until you pinpoint the culprit. This process of elimination can feel tedious, but it's often the quickest way to identify exactly which feature is causing conflicts.

RESOLVING AUTHENTICATION AND ACCESS ISSUES

Another dilemma I've seen is where users can't sign in or keep receiving "Unauthorized" messages. Start by confirming that their email address matches the one you're using for app permissions. If your app relies on domain-specific accounts (like a corporate domain), ensure the user belongs to that domain. Remember that changes to sign-in providers or subscription plans can disrupt existing user permissions, so a quick review of your security settings helps here.

Also, encourage your users to clear browser caches or app data if repeated login attempts fail. Sounds basic, but sometimes an outdated token or stale session triggers these headaches. I've solved more than one so-called "complex" issue simply by advising a user to clear their app cache and try again.

ADDRESSING FORMULA AND EXPRESSION CONFLICTS

When a formula doesn't produce the right outcome—or yields no outcome at all—it's time to scrutinize the Expression Assistant. Incorrect references, missing brackets, or referencing a non-existent column can invalidate your entire logic. One workaround I find helpful is to break larger expressions into smaller segments and test each component independently. This way, you see exactly where (and why) an expression isn't doing its job.

My best tip: Embrace simple test data. If your expression aims to calculate discounts, plug in easy numbers like 10 or 100, so you know instantly if the formula hits the mark. That immediate clarity shortens the debugging cycle.

FIXING INCONSISTENT VIEWS AND UX GLITCHES

Sometimes an app element vanishes or a view looks distorted, leaving users scratching their heads. Such display issues often trace back to a show-if or slice condition that accidentally filters out data crucial to the layout. Check your conditional expressions—did you specify a condition that inadvertently hides the entire table for certain user roles?

You can also replicate the user's experience by signing in under their role or account to see exactly what they see.

If the interface behaves erratically across different devices, investigate how the app scales to varying screen sizes. On smaller screens, certain elements may hide or condense. Try adjusting the "UX" → "Options" settings or ensure images and columns have appropriate display settings for mobile, tablet, and desktop modes.

UNRAVELING WORKFLOW HANG-UPS

When a workflow fails or doesn't trigger at the right time, I usually start with the workflow log. This record often reveals if the workflow is seeing your events and whether it's encountering any errors during execution. Common pitfalls include setting conditions too strictly (so it never fires) or referencing columns that don't exist or are spelled incorrectly.

It's also worth confirming that your plan supports the type of automation you need—some advanced workflows require higher-tier subscriptions. And if you're sending emails, check for spam folders or domain filters. I've had at least one scenario where test emails never arrived because our corporate mail system flagged them as spam, causing unnecessary confusion.

OVERCOMING APP DEPLOYMENT ROADBLOCKS

Occasionally, you'll face issues taking your app from prototype to a more formal deployment. Maybe certain user roles can't see the app in their launcher or you encounter domain-wide restrictions. Touch base with your IT or admin teams to confirm your domain policies. Additionally, double-check your deployment settings in the "Manage" → "Deployment" section—if your app is still marked as a prototype, some features might be limited or produce warning messages.

Hint: Keep notes on standard deployment steps, including verifying user shares, checking sign-in methods, and revisiting table permissions. This quick reference becomes a lifesaver when time is short and you need to roll out an update fast.

LEANING ON LOGS AND COMMUNITY SUPPORT

If all else fails and the issue feels beyond your scope, AppSheet's logs and the broader AppSheet community can be surprisingly helpful. The *Audit History* or *App Performance* logs frequently highlight the exact moment something misfires, offering clues to the root cause. And if you're stumped, the user forums or support channels often have encountered similar issues. Sometimes a quick search or post can point you to insights or a known bug with a documented workaround.

My personal approach: I make notes of each resolved hiccup—what triggered it, how I diagnosed it, and what solution actually worked. Over time, these entries form a personal playbook, sparing me from reinventing the wheel whenever a familiar glitch pops up.

GAINING CONFIDENCE THROUGH TROUBLESHOOTING

No one eagerly anticipates app emergencies, but over time, troubleshooting transforms from a stressful scramble into a methodical process that hones your skills. Each sticky situation you fix builds your confidence and sharpens your understanding of AppSheet's nuances. For me, that sense of mastery is part of what makes working with this platform so rewarding. You grasp not only how to build apps but also how to shepherd them through hiccups and back to smooth operation.

Final thought: A well-developed approach to problem-solving—gathering detailed info, isolating the source, and systematically testing solutions—carries over into any project you tackle in the future. By refining these techniques, you'll be better equipped than ever to maintain stable, reliable apps that stand the test of everyday use, no matter what surprises surface.

Chapter 24: Real-World Use Cases and Best Practices

LEVERAGING APPSHEET IN PRACTICAL ENVIRONMENTS

Welcome to this chapter, I remember the moment I realized that the true power of Google AppSheet wasn't just in personal or departmental apps—it was in how easily those apps could solve challenges across different industries and organizational sizes. After sharing a few of my prototypes with colleagues, I quickly saw how each situation called for unique perspectives on data collection, process automation, and user experience. In this chapter, let's dive into some real-world scenarios that showcase the best ways to make your AppSheet solutions thrive in diverse settings.

ADAPTING TO INDUSTRY-SPECIFIC WORKFLOWS

I've seen firsthand how AppSheet's flexibility benefits fields as varied as healthcare, logistics, and retail. In healthcare, for example, teams can track patient check-ins and procedure outcomes, ensuring accuracy and swift reporting without waiting on IT for a custom app.

Meanwhile, logistics companies use AppSheet to manage shipment schedules and routing, sending real-time updates to drivers' mobile devices. Even retail operations—both brick-and-mortar and online—lean on AppSheet for inventory checks, product restocking, and sales analytics.

Best Practice: Always start by mapping out the core workflows within your specific industry. Identify the essential data points, key pain areas, and how often tasks repeat. This blueprint guides your initial design, ensuring your final app directly addresses urgent real-world needs.

SUPPORTING FIELD TEAMS AND ON-SITE DATA CAPTURE

In many organizations, crucial data is gathered outside the confines of an office—think construction sites, client visits, or campus tours. AppSheet shines here by offering offline capabilities and mobile-friendly forms. I recall coaching a facility maintenance crew on how to log equipment status updates while hopping between multiple client sites. Instead of juggling paper notes, they tracked everything in one shared app, which auto-synced once they got back online.

Insight: If your teams frequently work in low-connectivity environments, focus on building robust offline functionality. That means limiting heavy images, using minimal data sets, and ensuring your forms still guide users properly without an active internet connection.

HANDLING CUSTOMER-FACING SOLUTIONS

It's exciting to see organizations use AppSheet as a channel for customer engagement. Once, I collaborated on an app that let clients book appointments, upload mandatory forms, and even chat with support—directly from their phones. Though AppSheet can't replace a fully custom-coded public platform, it holds its own for smaller-scale or niche customer-facing tasks.

Of course, greater exposure means heightened attention to security. You'll want to lock down parts of your database, ensure sensitive fields never appear in the wrong hands, and confirm that sign-in or access requirements meet your organization's standards.

Pro Tip: Keep things simple for external users. Limit the number of steps for sign-in or form entry, and visually mark essential tasks like "Submit Request" or "Edit Profile." A streamlined design can make all the difference in user adoption.

INTEGRATING APPSHEET WITH EXISTING SYSTEMS

One real-world scenario that often appears is the need to tie AppSheet apps into legacy or large-scale enterprise systems. I've witnessed teams bridge AppSheet forms to databases like MySQL or PostgreSQL for more robust reporting, or connect with Salesforce for streamlined lead tracking. Whenever you integrate, be clear on how often data should synchronize, what type of credentials are needed, and whether your organization's security policies allow external app connections.

Best Practice: Conduct a brief audit of existing data platforms and APIs before building out your app. Understanding which systems you can securely tap into keeps you from reinventing workflows or duplicating data storage.

AUTOMATING REPETITIVE TASKS FOR EFFICIENCY

I've seen orders processed, approvals granted, and compliance checks all run through automated workflows in AppSheet. One team I worked with reduced manual data entry by 70% simply by configuring triggers that fired whenever users updated a key field. Through these workflows, the app sent confirmations, updated spreadsheets, and notified the right manager with relevant info in one swift motion.

Going a step further, you can chain apps together—perhaps funneling new records from one department into another's queue. This synergy not only cuts down on errors but also encourages a culture where people trust the system to handle the mundane, freeing them to focus on strategic tasks.

Recommendation: Start small. Automate the one or two steps that consume most of your team's time, and measure the impact. With that success, you can expand to other tasks or more sophisticated logic without overwhelming users.

CRAFTING DASHBOARDS FOR DATA INSIGHTS

Data visibility is another realm where AppSheet shines. Whether it's sales metrics, project milestones, or compliance indicators, interactive dashboards transform dry numbers into actionable visuals. In one client-facing project, I watched sales reps update their pipeline in real time, pulling up clean charts that instantly revealed marketing campaign effectiveness. Instead of combing through hundreds of rows, decisions were informed by at-a-glance insights.

Keep in mind that a well-structured dashboard pairs charts or tables in a logical layout, so users see correlations without rummaging through multiple views. Encourage input from the data consumers themselves—understanding which numbers they monitor daily helps you tailor the final design.

Case in Point: A non-profit I partnered with relied on a single "Volunteer Dashboard" to track event attendance and donation collections. Feedback was immediate and comprehensive, facilitating swift improvements in volunteer allocation and fundraising strategies.

ENSURING LONG-TERM MAINTENANCE

Over time, even the most successful demos or pilot programs evolve into reliable, ever-present tools. While the initial setup might be quick, I've noticed that many best practices revolve around thoughtful upkeep. For instance, regularly archiving outdated data to prevent bloat, refining security permissions as user counts shift, and scheduling periodic sync tests all keep your app running at peak health.

It's also wise to document key aspects of your build—like naming conventions, workflows, or reference relationships. When new contributors join or your company merges with another, having clarity on these details shortens the learning curve and guards against unintentional changes in your data structure.

REFINING WHEN TO SCALE OR PRIORITIZE SPEED

As your solution matures, you'll sometimes face trade-offs between scaling for more users or optimizing speed for your current base. If your app aims to serve many departments across multiple regions, you might shift to more robust data sources or adopt slicing logic that includes role-specific filters. Conversely, if your user group stays compact but demands top-notch speed, you might invest in lighter interfaces or advanced sync settings.

The sweet spot depends on your app's purpose at any given moment. Over the years, I've learned to reevaluate these goals every few months—what worked for 50 users might not hold up when you approach 500 or 5,000.

LEARNING FROM COMPLETED PROJECTS

One of the joys of working with so many AppSheet use cases is seeing patterns that rarely change: the power of incremental improvements, the necessity of user-centered testing, and the huge benefits of involving the right stakeholders early. Revision after revision, I've watched teams refine both data flows and user experiences until they felt nearly effortless.

If you ever feel stuck or ponder whether AppSheet can handle a certain use case, seek examples from the vibrant user community or your organization's app builders. There's a good chance someone has tackled a similar challenge—be it scanning barcodes for inventory, capturing images for inspections, or auto-calculating timesheets—and carved a path you can adapt to your unique needs.

NURTURING A BEST-PRACTICE MINDSET

Regardless of industry or application size, the best results come from approaching each new request with a sense of curiosity and a willingness to iterate. Here are a few reminders I return to often:

- **Start Simple:** Build a lean proof-of-concept and refine based on user input.
- **Communicate Constantly:** Keep stakeholders updated, and integrate feedback swiftly.
- **Watch Your Data:** Ensure columns and references are consistent, secure, and archivable.
- **Celebrate Milestones:** Recognize each successful rollout or feature upgrade—it motivates everyone involved.

Final Reflection: Many real-world wins come from pairing an everyday process (like tracking, approving, or managing) with a structured, user-friendly AppSheet experience. Once the data flows smoothly and tasks feel automated, you'll likely find your team can tackle bigger objectives with newfound efficiency.

www.ingramcontent.com/pod-product-compliance
Lightning Source LLC
LaVergne TN
LVHW051239050326
832903LV00028B/2477